MUST KNOW

HIGH SCHOOL COMPUTER PROGRAMMING

Julie Sway

D1534457

Mc
Graw
Hill

New York   Chicago   San Francisco   Athens   London   Madrid
Mexico City   Milan   New Delhi   Singapore   Sydney   Toronto

1 2 3 4 5 6 7 8 9   LCR   24 23 22 21 20 19

ISBN   978-1-260-45846-6
MHID   1-260-45846-6

e-ISBN   978-1-260-45847-3
e-MHID   1-260-45847-3

Interior design by Steve Straus of Think Book Works.
Cover and letter art by Kate Rutter.

McGraw-Hill Education books are available at special quantity discounts to use as premiums and sales promotions or for use in corporate training programs. To contact a representative, please visit the Contact Us pages at www.mhprofessional.com.

Contents

21 Projects

22 Micro:bit

Introduction

Welcome to your new computer programming book! Let us try to explain why we believe you've made the right choice. This probably isn't your first rodeo with either a textbook or other kind of guide to a school subject. You've probably had your fill of books asking you to memorize lots of terms (such is school). This book isn't going to do that—although you're welcome to memorize anything you take an interest in. You may also have found that a lot of books jump the gun and make a lot of promises about all the things you'll be able to accomplish by the time you reach the end of a given chapter. In the process, those books can make you feel as though you missed out on the building blocks that you actually need to master those goals.

With *Must Know High School Computer Programming,* we've taken a different approach. When you start a new chapter, right off the bat you will immediately see one or more **must know** ideas. These are the essential concepts behind what you are going to study, and they will form the foundation of what you will learn throughout the chapter. With these **must know** ideas, you will have what you need to hold it together as you study, and they will be your guide as you make your way through each chapter.

To build on this foundation, you will find easy-to-follow discussions of the topic at hand, accompanied by comprehensive examples that show you how to apply what you're learning to solving typical computer programming questions. Each chapter ends with review questions—more than 250 throughout the book— designed to instill confidence as you practice your new skills.

This book has other features that will help you on this computer programming journey of yours. It has a number of sidebars that will both help provide helpful information or just serve as a quick break from your studies. The **BTW** sidebars ("by the way") point out important information as well as tell you what to be careful about programming-wise. Every once in a while, an **IRL** sidebar ("in real life") will tell you what you're studying has to do with the real world; other IRLs may just be interesting factoids.

In addition, this book is accompanied by a flashcard app that will give you the ability to test yourself at any time. The app includes more than 100 "flashcards" with a review question on one "side" and the answer on the other. You can either work through the flashcards by themselves or use them alongside the book. To find out where to get the app and how to use it, go to the next section, The Flashcard App.

Before you get started, though, let me introduce you to your guide throughout this book. Julie Sway works as the Technology Department Chair and Education Technology and Innovation Director at Brookstone School, in Columbus, Georgia, and has taught AP Computer Science A and AP Computer Science Principles. Not only that, Julie has served as a reader of the AP Computer Science Principles performance tasks.

She has a clear idea about what you should get out of a computer course and has developed strategies to help you get there. Julie has also seen the kinds of trouble that students can run into, and she is an experienced hand at solving those difficulties. In this book, she applies that experience both to showing you the most effective way to learn a given concept as well as how to extricate yourself from traps you may have fallen into. She will be a trustworthy guide as you expand your programming knowledge and develop new skills.

Before we leave you to Julie's surefooted guidance, let us give you one piece of advice. While we know that saying something "is the *worst*" is a cliché, if anything *is* the worst in computer programming, it may be having to learn a programming language. Let Julie introduce you to the concepts and show you how to apply them confidently to your computer programming work. Take our word for it, mastering a programming language will leave you in good stead for the rest of your computer career.

Good luck with your studies!

The Editors at McGraw-Hill

The Flashcard App

This book features a bonus flashcard app. It will help you test yourself on what you've learned as you make your way through the book (or in and out). It includes 100-plus "flashcards," both "front" and "back." It gives you two options as to how to use it. You can jump right into the app and start from any point that you want. Or you can take advantage of the handy QR Codes near the end of each chapter in the book; they will take you directly to the flashcards related to what you're studying at the moment.

To take advantage of this bonus feature, follow these easy steps:

Search for **Must Know High School** App from
either Google Play or the App Store.

↓

Download the app to your smartphone or tablet.

↓

Once you've got the app,
you can use it in either of two ways.

↙   ↘

Just open the app and you're ready to go.	Use your phone's QR code reader to scan any of the book's QR codes.
You can start at the beginning, or select any of the chapters listed.	You'll be taken directly to the flashcards that match your chapter of choice.

↘   ↙

Get ready to test your programming knowledge!

Author's Note

Technology has permeated your life, and now you want to know a little more about it! Maybe you have a great idea for an app, and need to know how to get started. Or you have always wanted a personal robot assistant and need to know how to program it. This book is the place to get you started.

Technology has integrated itself into many aspects of our lives. There are few jobs that do not have a technology-related component, so the more you know, the more valuable you can be to an employer, even if you are not a programmer. Knowing how software is developed helps you be a better client and better identify the software requirements you need the project team to develop and deliver.

Many schools, districts, and even states are starting to offer and even require students to take a computer science course as a graduation requirement. Many students (and adults) are uneasy about taking their first course. Let me assure you, computer science is not that hard! You just haven't had any exposure to it yet. Our first year of school, we begin to build the fundamentals of reading and math with learning our letters and numbers. That continues throughout school! The good news is that there is some overlap with math and logic concepts that you may have already learned, and since you are likely older than a kindergarten student, you will be able to grasp the concepts and progress through the material presented here at a reasonable pace.

While each high school has its own curriculum and pathway for programming, there are several courses that many schools have that someone who uses this book would be well prepared to take. These include introductory courses in any programming language as well as Game Design and Development and Robotics. The fundamental concepts covered here, along with critical thinking, logic application, and problem solving, apply to any programming language and are just implemented a little differently in various ones. Some introductory courses use block-based programming that use the same basic concepts and just do a little more of the programming work behind the scenes. Students still perform "real programming" with these languages. Students who take either or both of the College Board–offered Advanced Placement–level courses in Computer Science would benefit from this book through the structure and concepts covered. The basic concepts that apply to programming are covered here, and those are what make this book a helpful tool to learning other programming languages in a variety of courses.

So whether you want to learn basic concepts before your first high school–level programming course or are just interested in learning more on your own, the first step is finding a resource like this book. Join in and try to create the code in the examples. Just as with any new skill, you cannot be a programmer by simply reading about it. You need to have hands-on experience coding too!

Hardware and Software

MUST KNOW

 Computer software runs on hardware. The basic hardware structure has input, output, a CPU, and memory.

 Everything connects to the motherboard.

hile this is a book to get you started with programming, it helps to understand the basics of hardware too. The physical components of a computer are the hardware. Your programs cannot run without hardware, whether it is a desktop, laptop, mobile device, or other type of hardware device. While there is a lot of detail engineered into hardware, the basic structure is essentially the same.

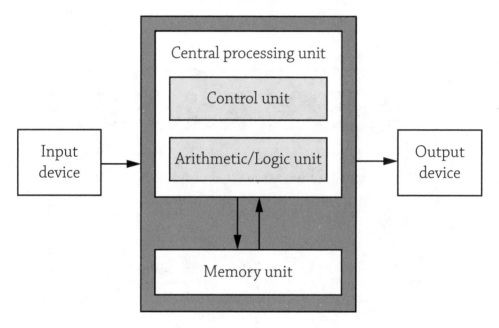

Von Neumann Architecture

Input devices are used to get data into the computer. Examples of input are mouse clicks, screen taps, swipes, typing from a keyboard, and audio from microphones, among others. Output can be sent to device screens, speakers, headphones, and printers, including 3D printers. There are other types, but these examples are fairly common for our world today.

Input and output devices connect wirelessly or with cables to the main computing device.

Motherboard

Inside the computer is the **CPU**, which stands for **central processing unit**. It contains the **control unit** that manages instructions and the **arithmetic/logic unit** that handles math calculations and the logic for programs. You'll sometimes hear the CPU referred to as the brain of the computer, because it directs all the processing. The **memory unit** stores the information and instructions for programs that are currently running. You may have heard the term **RAM**, which stands for **random access memory**. RAM is internal to the device. It does not permanently store data and loses what was stored in it when the computer is turned off, making RAM a volatile form of memory.

A computer's hard drive stores programs and files of all types such as images, videos, and documents. The hard drive can hold much more data than RAM. You can also purchase external hard drives and use flash drives to permanently store data. You may have heard of the motherboard. It connects everything! This includes any external input or output devices such as a printer. The CPU resides on the motherboard, too, as does the RAM.

REVIEW QUESTIONS

1. What are the basic components of hardware?

2. How are input and output devices connected to hardware?

3. What is the role of the memory unit?

4. What does it mean to say RAM is volatile?

5. What is the CPU sometimes called?

A Computer's Favorite Language – Binary!

5

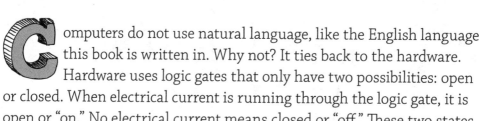omputers do not use natural language, like the English language this book is written in. Why not? It ties back to the hardware. Hardware uses logic gates that only have two possibilities: open or closed. When electrical current is running through the logic gate, it is open or "on." No electrical current means closed or "off." These two states, on and off, easily convert to a value of 0 (no current) or 1 (current), which are the values used with **binary**: 0 and 1. It would be far more difficult to consistently measure different voltage amounts to represent more numbers. Current or no current is reliable. There are millions, if not billions, of logic gates in a typical computing device such as a laptop or smartphone.

So, we know why we use binary, but how do a bunch of 0s and 1s represent words, numbers, and symbols? Excellent question! A binary number can represent multiple pieces of information, such as a number, text, color, or sound, among others. The software being used knows how to interpret that binary number for its use. For example, image editing software would interpret the binary number as a color. Music software would interpret the same binary combination as a sound. For example, the binary number 01000001 can be, among other things:

> 65
> capital A
> color fuchsia

Let's take a number in our normal decimal number system and convert it to binary. Think of a number between 1 and 10. I'll choose 7. Now, think of how many ways you can represent 7 of something. Here are a few:

> 7, seven, siete, VII

Each one represents the same amount. We can also use different number systems to represent the same "amount" of something.

Place Value

Our number system uses ten numbers, 0–9. Here's a flash back to elementary school math. When you need the number 10, you have to "carry over" to the "tens" column and use two numbers to represent it. You have 1 ten and 0 ones.

tens	ones
1	0

When we need to represent the number 321, we have to carry over to a third column to the left, which is our hundreds column.

10^2	10^1	10^0
hundreds	tens	ones
3	2	1

Notice across the top of each column, we have the number 10 raised to a power. We use the number 10 in this case, because that is our number system. It's also called base 10 because we have 10 numbers in it. Remember that 0 is a valid number and our numbers in base 10 are 0, 1, 2, 3, 4, 5, 6, 7, 8, 9.

The exponents always start at 0 for the ones column. Remember from your math class that any number raised to the power 0 is the value 1.

$$10^0 = 1$$

→ The tens column is 10^1, which is $10 \times 1 = 10$.
→ The hundreds column is 10^2, which is $10 \times 10 = 100$.

Do you see the pattern with the base and exponents? What would the thousands column be?

Binary Numbers Place Value

As we said earlier, binary numbers only use 0 and 1. Therefore, we also call this the base 2 number system. We will use the same principles with base 2 (binary) that we did with base 10 (decimal).

Say we start counting with 0, then 1. When we want to represent two of something, we don't have a number for it, so we have to create a new column, the twos.

twos	ones
1	0

So, in binary, the number to represent two is 10_2. Notice the subscript of 2 indicating that this is the number system base 2.

To continue with our counting in binary, to represent three, we would have 1 two and 1 one:

twos	ones
1	1

Three in binary is: 11_2.

To summarize, for place value, instead of ones, tens, and hundreds, we have ones, twos, fours, and so on.

When we get to four, we have run out of space using only two numbers, so we need a new column.

2^2	2^1	2^0
fours	twos	ones
1	0	0

Notice across the top of each column, we are using the same pattern as we did with base 10. We use the number 2 as the base, because that is our number system. The exponents always start at 0 for the ones column. Again, any number raised to the power 0 is the value 1.

$$2^0 = 1$$

$\rightarrow$ The twos column is 2^1, which is $2 \times 1 = 2$.
$\rightarrow$ The fours column is 2^2, which is $2 \times 2 = 4$.

Do you see the pattern with the base and exponents? What would the next column be?

Each digit in binary is called a **bit**, which is short for binary digit. Eight bits make a byte.

Let's build our "twos" table for a byte.

2^7	2^6	2^5	2^4	2^3	2^2	2^1	2^0
128	64	32	16	8	4	2	1

BTW

I have always thought that the person who created these terms was hungry at the time, because 4 bits is called a, nybble.

The second row is the value of 2 raised to the exponent.

Each column to the left represents an increasing power of 2, which doubles the column to the right of it.

Converting Decimal Numbers to Binary

To convert a decimal number to binary, use the following algorithm with the previous twos table.

1. Write down your decimal number.

2. Subtract from your decimal number the largest decimal number in the binary table that you can without getting a negative result.

3. Mark a one in the column on the table for the power of 2 you subtracted.

4. Mark a zero in the columns that could not be subtracted and were skipped.

5. Repeat steps 1–4 until your decimal value reaches zero.

6. Note: Use leading zeroes on the left to make a full byte (8 bits.)

Let's look at an example.

EXAMPLE

▶ Convert 42 to binary.

▶ Let's start by creating our twos table.

2^7	2^6	2^5	2^4	2^3	2^2	2^1	2^0
128	64	32	16	8	4	2	1
0	0	1	0	1	0	1	0

▶ Starting from the leftmost column, the first number you can subtract from 42 without having a negative result is 32. Place 0 in each column to the left of 2^5 and 1 in the column for 2^5.

$$42 - 32 = 10$$

▶ Take the number left after subtracting and find the next number in the table that can be subtracted without resulting in a negative number.

▶ We cannot subtract 16 from 10, so place 0 in the 2^4 column.

▶ We can subtract 8, so place 1 in the 2^3 column.

$$10 - 8 = 2$$

▶ You cannot subtract 4, so place 0 in the 2^2 column.

▶ You can subtract 2, so place 1 in the 2^1 column.

$$2 - 2 = 0$$

▶ We are at 0 and do not need to subtract anything else. However, we need to make sure we don't forget to place 0 in the 2^0 column:

$$42_{10} = 00101010_2$$

Let's try another one, using a larger number. Remember the steps to convert it are the same!

EXAMPLE

▶ Convert 73 to binary.

▶ Create the twos table.

2^7	2^6	2^5	2^4	2^3	2^2	2^1	2^0
128	64	32	16	8	4	2	1
0	1	0	0	1	0	0	1

▶ Find the largest number we can subtract from 73 without having a negative number as the result.

▶ That would be 2^6 or 64.

$$73 - 64 = 9$$

▶ Place 0 in the 2^7 column.

▶ Place 1 in the 2^6 column.

▶ Place 0 in the 2^5 and 2^4 columns because subtracting those values would result in a negative number.

$$9 - 8 = 1$$

▶ Place 1 in the 2^3 column.

▶ Place 0 in the 2^2 and 2^1 columns.

$$1 - 1 = 0$$

▶ Place 1 in the 2^0 column.

$$01001001_2 = 73_{10}$$

Converting Binary Numbers to Decimal

Sometimes, we want to do the opposite conversion, from a binary number to a decimal one.

1. Write the binary table as we did in the examples above with each bit of the binary number in the appropriate column.

2. For columns that have 1 in them, add the values of the power of 2. (You are multiplying 1 times the value of the power of 2 in each column.)

3. The total of all columns with a 1 in them equals the decimal value equivalent.

Let's try that out.

▶ Let's convert 10110110_2 to decimal. First, let's build the table and place each bit in its correct column:

2^7	2^6	2^5	2^4	2^3	2^2	2^1	2^0
128	64	32	16	8	4	2	1
1	0	1	1	0	1	1	0

▶ We are adding the values of each column multiplied together:

$(128 \times 1) + (64 \times 0) + (32 \times 1) + (16 \times 1) + (8 \times 0) + (4 \times 1) + (2 \times 1) + (1 \times 0) = 128 + 0 + 32 + 16 + 0 + 4 + 2 + 0 = 182_{10}$

BTW

Any time you have a binary number that is made up of all 1s on its right, the number in decimal is always 1 less than the next power of 2. Logically, this makes sense, since you cannot have the number 2 in binary. The next value would need a new column and would be the next power of 2. For example:

$00001111_2 = 15_{10}$ because the next value in the chart would be 2^4, or 16.

$00011111_2 = 31_{10}$ because the next column is 2^5, or 32.

$11111111_2 = 255$ because the next column is 2^8, or 256.

The table on the next page shows the equivalent decimal and binary values for 0 to 16. Notice the pattern of the binary numbers as they increase. For the binary numbers, the rightmost value of the numbers, the ones place value, flips between 0 and 1 as the decimal number increases by 1. The next number to the left, the twos place value, flips after the decimal number increases by two: 0, 0, 1, 1. This pattern continues with the fours column with the binary value changing between 0 and 1 when the decimal number increases by 4. The pattern, based on the value of 2 raised to the exponent, continues with each of the place value columns.

decimal	binary
0	00000000
1	00000001
2	00000010
3	00000011
4	00000100
5	00000101
6	00000110
7	00000111
8	00001000
9	00001001
10	00001010
11	00001011
12	00001100
13	00001101
14	00001110
15	00001111
16	00010000

REVIEW QUESTIONS

1. Why do computers use the binary number system?

2. What is a bit?

3. What is a byte?

4. What does place value mean with binary?

5. Convert 23 to binary.

6. Convert 121 to binary.

7. Convert 99 to binary.

8. Convert 01010011_2 to decimal.

9. Convert 01101011_2 to decimal.

10. Convert 11000011_2 to decimal.

Getting Started

MUST ⚡ KNOW

⚡ We write code using high-level programming languages.

⚡ Compilers and interpreters convert program code to machine code (binary) for the computer to execute.

⚡ The iterative development process helps programmers design and create software that meets given requirements.

⚡ The iterative process involves multiple occurrences of designing, coding, and testing the software.

Code can have different meanings depending on your point of view. Most often, **code** is referred to as a program written in a programming language that people can run to do something. People might refer to it as "This is my code" or "I wrote this code." No kidding, right? There are many programming languages available to use, and more are being developed all the time. Wikipedia lists over 700 different programming languages with new ones being released almost daily.

Code is also the language a computer can understand. Programs are usually written in high-level, "English-like" (or other natural language) programming languages. These are much easier for people to learn and use. These programs need to be translated to **machine language** so the computer can understand it. As discussed in the previous chapter, computers use binary code, a base 2 number system that consists of zeros and ones. Binary code is what computers use to actually execute the programs we write.

In this book, we will use the Python programming language, which is commonly used by many businesses and software developers today. Python is used by Google, YouTube, and DropBox, among many other companies.

IRL Guido van Rossum, a native of the Netherlands, created Python and released the first version in 1991. It is named Python not for the reptile, but because van Rossum was a fan of the British comedy group Monty Python. There are references to the group scattered throughout the documentation.

In July 2018, Guido van Rossum retired from his role as Python's "Benevolent Dictator for Life," which had given him the final say about changes to Python and the settling of disagreements among developers of the open-source software.

Compilers and interpreters are used by high-level programming languages to convert the source code to machine language. Essentially, compilers and interpreters enable the computers to read and execute the code written by a programmer.

The difference between compilers and interpreters is that compilers translate all the code and create an executable file while interpreters translate the program code to machine code line by line as the program runs. Compilers are faster, but the difference, especially with small programs or using them with smaller amounts of data, is often negligible. Python uses an interpreter.

BTW

In the past, compilers and interpreters used to convert the programming code to Assembly language for the computer being used. (Assembly languages are not binary but use instructions that are much less like native language and are specific to the machine in use.) Assembly languages "assembled" the pieces and kept track of many aspects of executing the code. Nowadays, many compilers still have an option to generate assembly code rather than binary.

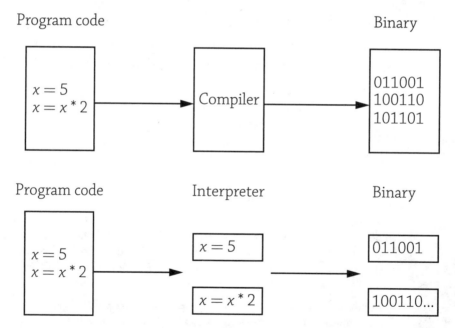

A compiler converts the entire program to binary in an executable file. Interpreters convert a program to binary line by line. This is also a good time to learn that, in programming languages, an asterisk means multiplication.

IRL Many email systems do not allow executable files as attachments because malware, could be embedded in it. It's a good idea to run an executable file through antivirus software before using it to detect any malware.

If you receive an email with an attachment in executable format that you are not expecting, either contact the person who sent it in a separate message, if you know the sender, or just delete it.

Iterative Software Development

Good software development doesn't happen by luck. There is a process involved to help ensure programmers develop accurate, efficient, and readable code. There are a multitude of development processes, and a key factor is that software development is an **iterative process** (cyclical), as the diagram below shows.

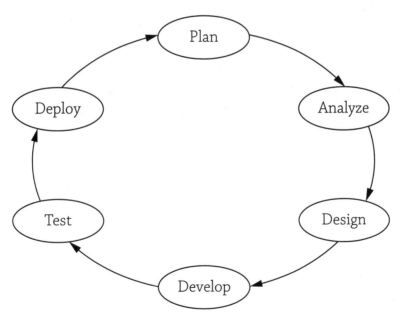

Software Development Life Cycle

When we want to start writing a program, unless it is a small, simple program, we are not able to just sit down and start writing the code. We first have to ensure we understand the requirements of the problem or need that the software is supposed to solve. The **analyze** section of the development life cycle addresses this.

 **IRL** Many times, especially for large or complex software projects, all the requirements are not known right at the beginning. You sometimes have to move on to the next stage and move back to the Analyze requirements stage several times as more information becomes to refine the requirements. It could also be a case of technology not being able to handle the client's request and having to adjust the requirements.

We then have to think it through and really figure out what we want our program to do first. This is the **software design** stage. Good programmers take the time to do this step, because they produce much better code as a result. Most businesses and organizations require this and will have reviews of the design and sign off on it before coding begins. Part of this process is **decomposition**, which is breaking a programming solution into smaller segments that can be easily understood for coding purposes. These smaller modules can then be combined into the larger project solution. Only then do we begin to write and test our code in the Develop stage.

As you are writing the code, you are expected to test and fix any program errors in your code. This is called **unit testing**. Once the software is working as expected, it needs to be thoroughly tested. **Integration testing** checks to be sure all the different sections of code work together, and then **System testing** checks the entire system functionality. There are several famous instances where testing did not find errors.

IRL In 1999, a Mars Probe crashed on the surface of Mars. The investigation into the crash revealed that calculations were made in inches by one team and centimeters by another team. Testing did not find the error, and the end result was the probe being destroyed when it entered the Mars atmosphere and tried to land.

There are also well-defined processes for testing software. If you are writing software programs for an organization or to sell, you should use these steps to help ensure your software works consistently and correctly every time it runs. The testing steps do not assume the code works correctly and looks for errors or ways to make the program crash. It's far better for that to happen before others are using it:

- After errors are identified, the process starts again.

- You design solutions to the bugs found, refine the requirements, program the updates, and retest.

- This repeats until all known bugs have been corrected and tested.

- The software is not deployed until all requirements have been met and **user tested** and reliably working. Then it can be deployed out to users or placed in the marketplace for free or for a fee.

Ask a friend to test your code. They will be happy to try and break it for you! They won't know how it is supposed to work, so you'll get better tested code as a result.

We can compare this to deciding you want to drive from Florida to New York. While it is possible to jump in the car and start driving without a map or GPS and still get there, your route is likely to have some wrong turns, U-turns, rush hour traffic, and other mishaps, such as construction or not knowing where gas stations are to fill up the car's gasoline tank, and your energy tank too!

You will most likely have a shorter, cheaper, more efficient, and more enjoyable trip if you take some time to plan it out first.

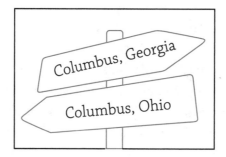

Without planning, where will you end up?

The same process applies to writing code. You can get a program to work if you sit down and write code without thinking it through first. However, if you take the time to design a solution, your code will likely be shorter, more efficient, more readable, more complete, more reliable, and it will take less time to create with fewer errors because you did not forget to include features and have to work them in later. There will also be much less frustration for the programmer—you! Spending the time in advance to design a good solution saves a lot of time when actually writing the code.

With larger projects, you may be part of a project team. Multiple people may be writing sections of code that then all need to work together seamlessly. Without understanding the requirements and creating the design prior to coding, it would be difficult and time-consuming to get different programs communicating and well integrated.

Another benefit of the iterative development process is that once a block of code is working, you can set it aside and develop another section of code. These stand-alone sections of code can be shared among the project team and used as often as needed in the project code. As more modules are developed, be sure to test the connections between any modules that work together or share data.

This process is an effective way to develop good software, whether it is for your personal use, for an organization's use, or for sale on the app store or playground for anyone to install.

REVIEW QUESTIONS

1. What "language" do computers use?

2. How does program code get from a natural language programming language to machine code?

3. How do compilers differ from interpreters?

4. Does a compiler or interpreter run faster?

5. Why should we use a software development process?

6. What is decomposition in programming terms?

7. Why is an iterative process used?

8. What is the design stage?

9. What type of testing should you conduct before publishing your software for others to use?

10. What would you be doing if you were conducting integration testing?

Flashcard App

Designing a Programming Solution: Algorithms

MUST KNOW

- Algorithms are a set of steps to do something, such as solve a problem or meet a request.

- Algorithms need to be specific. While people can infer or make reasonable assumptions, a computer cannot, so algorithms need to be detailed and very specific.

- There is almost always more than one right way to write an algorithm to meet the needed requirements.

n algorithm is a set of steps to do something. That "something" could be anything, such as a recipe for making your favorite dessert.

Recipes are the best kind of algorithm!

In programming, an algorithm provides the steps identified to solve a programming challenge. For example, the requirements could be to create a new digital basketball game application, or "app." It could be software to scan in price tags to calculate sales and update inventory. It could be tracking endangered sea turtle nests or coordinating traffic light cycles on city streets. In other words, algorithms help us do just about everything.

 **IRL** Two frequently used algorithms are sorting and searching algorithms. Organizations collect far more data than humans can process, and computers are perfect for this. Sorting algorithms put data in order, usually from smallest to largest. Searching algorithms try to find items in the data. There are many algorithms and software already written and tested for both searching and sorting.

An **algorithm** results from a programmer, first, working to understand the programming need and, second, breaking it down (or **decomposing** it) into manageable chunks to be coded.

Software can be decomposed into stand-alone sections that work together to create the complete solution.

Software projects can have one section or many sections of code that all work together to meet the customer's requirements.

If you are writing the code for someone, you will want the client to review the algorithm before you start programming, because you may have missed something. Also, the client you are writing the code for could have new information that was not available previously. That always helps! It is also possible that the client may have changed his or her mind about certain aspects of the project. Something external to your project, such as tax laws, may have changed that will require a change to the algorithm. You have a better chance of hitting the target with your project if you get your design reviewed and approved before coding.

If you are writing the code for yourself or a group of friends, then it is still a good idea to go over your plan before coding, but it is less important if the program is just for your own use for fun, rather than something someone pays money for others to use.

IRL Brute-force algorithms are used to try to guess passwords or crack the secret key used to encrypt information like financial or personal data.

Here's how we might write an algorithm to make a peanut butter and jelly sandwich. Try to follow the algorithm and see if you think it is specific and accurate enough.

1. Get two slices of bread.

2. Get the peanut butter jar.

3. Open the peanut butter jar.

4. Scoop out a large portion of peanut butter.

5. Spread the peanut butter on one slice of bread.

6. Open the jelly jar.

7. Scoop out a moderate portion of jelly.

8. Spread the jelly on the other slice of bread.

9. Place the two slices of bread together, peanut butter side to jelly side.

10. Eat!

What's your algorithm to make a peanut butter and jelly sandwich?

Do you think there are any problems with the algorithm? Would you ask for more details anywhere? Are there improvements in the instructions that could be made?

Of course, the real question is whether you place the jelly on top of the peanut butter or on the other slice of bread! This demonstrates that there is almost always more than one right way to write an algorithm. Some algorithms may be more efficient than others, but they can all produce correct results.

IRL There are problems for which no algorithm can be written for all cases (at least so far). These are called **Undecidable Algorithms**. There are several famous ones, such as the Turing problem.

There are problems for which an algorithm can be written, but they would take too long to run for large datasets with our current computer processing capability. These are called **Intractable Algorithms**. Some of these are used for encrypting our data online so we can do things like send private messages and shop online with a credit card. In this case, intractability is a good thing!

EXAMPLE

▶ In my programming classes, I have students randomly pick a slip of paper with the name of an object on it. They have to write the algorithm to draw the object. Someone else in class then follows the instructions to see if they get the same shape. Here is one example. See what object you draw when you follow the instructions.

1. Draw a semicircle with the flat part facing down.

2. Draw a stick or rod coming from the bottom of the semicircle.

3. Draw a curved part on the bottom of the stick

4. Draw curved lines coming from the top of the semicircle and curving out toward the closest corner.

▶ It is not as easy as it sounds when you have to be specific and precise and cannot explain your instructions if someone has a question!

REVIEW QUESTIONS

1. What is an algorithm?

2. Is an algorithm written in a programming language?

3. Why do algorithms need to be specific?

4. Write an algorithm to open your device and enter a passcode. Include what happens if an incorrect passcode is entered. Also include what happens if an incorrect passcode is entered too many times.

5. Write an algorithm to draw a football goalpost and have a friend or family member follow it to see if it produces what you described. You can also come back to it in a day or two and follow the instructions yourself to see if you would change anything.

6. Follow this algorithm to draw an object. Make suggestions for more detailed instructions as needed.
    a. Draw two circles.
    b. Connect them at the top.
    c. Do a round thing on each side.
    d. Draw a hump at the top.
    e. Connect the round humps on the side with the one at the top.

Flashcard App

5 Pseudocode and Flowcharts

MUST ⚡ KNOW

⚡ Pseudocode is a combination of natural language (English in our case) and a programming language.

⚡ Pseudocode cannot run on a computer.

⚡ Flowcharts diagram the algorithm to be programmed.

⚡ Pseudocode and flowcharts help the software developer create a better program design.

o far, we have the requirements that our program code needs to solve, and we have designed an algorithm that can do it. Now it is time to start the process of translating these into software. We have two methods that are commonly used: pseudocode and flowcharting.

Pseudocode

Pseudocode is not a programming language, and a computer cannot run it. It is a combination of natural language (English in this book) and a programming language. As you create your program design, you may find you start to use pseudocode without even realizing it. Your pseudocode may initially be more English than programming language. As you learn more about programming and a specific programming language, you will naturally incorporate more programming lingo into your pseudocode. Pseudocode generally follows the structure of a program.

IRL Writing pseudocode and flowcharting are more casual in many organizations today. Programmers or teams may sketch out the pseudocode and/or flowchart as part of their design process, but it is not formally reviewed. Some organizations and government contracts, however, require a formal review process.

Here is an example of pseudocode that is more natural language than code:

EXAMPLE

▶ Check movie listings online

Is there a movie you want to see – yes / no
if no, find something else to do
end

If yes, is it showing at time can see it – yes / no
if no, find something else to do
end

If yes, find a ride

get money
go to movie
end

Here is another pseudocode example that is provided twice. The first time, it has more natural language, and the second time, it has more programming language incorporated into it.

EXAMPLE

▶ # More natural language – pseudocode

Select the house temperature setting for a weekday versus the evening versus the weekend during hot weather.

For the time of day and day of the week
        If room temperature is greater than thermostat setting + 3
            Turn on air conditioner
Repeat

▶ # Adding programming language components – pseudocode

get time_of_day
get day_of_week
get temp_set

repeat
        read current_temp
        if current_temp > temp_set + 3
            turn_on_ac

Flowcharts

Flowcharts serve a similar purpose to pseudocode. These diagram an algorithm rather than describing it in written form. Many people prefer a visual representation over a written one and may sketch out the flow of the algorithm.

The shapes used with flowcharts have set meanings. Here are a few basic shapes that can be used to define simple algorithms.

Start/end ⬭ This shape is used at the beginning and end of each flowchart.

Input/output ▱ Use this shape anytime data comes into or goes out of a step.

Process ▭ This shape is for actions that occur.

Decision ◇ Decisions in programs only have a "yes" or "no" outcome.

Flowchart shapes are connected by arrows. Only a decision will have more than one arrow coming out of it, one for the yes outcome and one arrow for the no outcome.

I often start my students off with an example they are very familiar with: waking up to an alarm on a school day. Here is an example of a flowchart of this process we created in class one day.

▶ We started at the top of the whiteboard with a small oval and wrote "start" in it.

(start)

▶ Students usually say they would be sleeping soundly, very typical for many teenagers, when suddenly, the alarm starts blasting! We have a good discussion about whether the alarm sounding should be considered an input or a process. We then add a shape for the process and label it.

Alarm goes off!

▶ Now we have a decision to make. Should we get out of bed or hit the snooze button on our alarm? Notice our decision can only have two outcomes: yes or no. This could also be a true or false outcome.

▶ If the answer to our question about being ready to roll out of bed is yes, then we need a process block for this.

Get out of bed

▶ If the answer to our question is no, we are not ready to wake up, then we need a process to hit the snooze alarm.

Hit snooze alarm

▶ These steps of the alarm going off and hitting the snooze alarm could repeat multiple times. Therefore, we want to place our process in the diagram where it is easy to show this repetition.

▶ Finally, at some point, we will have to get out of bed, so we can end our flowchart with another oval with "end" written in it.

end

▶ I usually wait to place the arrows after I have all my other steps identified. Sometimes, I will move the shapes around so it is easier to view, and I do not have arrows crossing each other.

Below is the final outcome from one class.

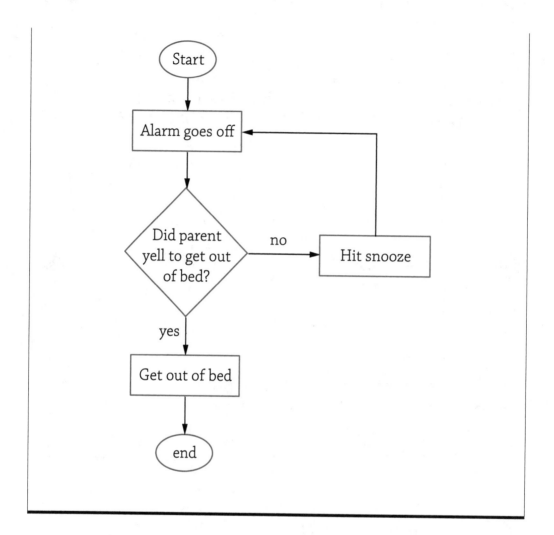

REVIEW QUESTIONS

1. What is pseudocode?

2. Why do we use it?

3. Can a computer run pseudocode?

4. Why are flowcharts used?

5. Can you use any shape in a flowchart?

6. Create a flowchart to pour a bowl of cereal with milk.

7. Write the pseudocode for dispensing an item from a vending machine.

8. Create a flowchart to dispense an item from a vending machine (same as the above pseudocode).

Writing and Commenting Our First Program

Where do we write software? There are many online editors available to write, test, and run code at no cost. You can open a web browser and use a search engine to find "online code editor" or "online ide."

Several results will be displayed from your search for you to evaluate. Two online editors I have used are repl.it and trinket.io. You can also download an IDE provided by the programming language or an external company to your computer and code, test it, and run programs from there. PyCharm is an IDE written specifically for Python that many developers use for both personal and professional purposes.

This book will use general terms that apply to many programming languages and provide examples in the Python programming language. You can use an online editor or the Python IDE, called IDLE. I always have my students download the latest version of the Python IDLE to their device. There are Mac, Linux, and Windows versions available. This is because I always want them to be able to work on their programs, even if the wireless network is slow or not working at all. If you have reliable Wi-Fi access, then an online editor may be fine for you, but it never hurts to be familiar with Python's IDLE.

> **BTW**
>
> **IDE** stands for **Integrated Development Environment.** IDEs generally provide a place for programmers to write code, a compiler or interpreter to check for syntax errors and create machine code, and debugging help.

IRL Python creator Guido von Rossum was, as we've seen, a huge Monty Python fan. IDLE, Python's IDE, was named after Monty Python member Eric Idle.

To download the latest version of Python 3 to your computer:

- Go to www.python.org/downloads/.

- Double-click on the download to install it.

- Make sure you download Python3 rather than Python2.

> **BTW**
>
> If you are using an online editor, usually both Python3 and Python2 are available. This book uses Python3. Python2 will no longer be supported after 2020, so go ahead and only learn Python3.

Let's Write Our First Program

Printing the phrase "Hello, world" has become a tradition for a first program in a new programming language. This is a simple way to test that the software is working properly on your device and an easy way to get started with a new language. Let's continue the tradition!

```
Hello, world
```

Open the Python 3 IDLE. The IDLE that comes with Python opens in "shell" mode where you will see the `>>>` prompt. This is useful for quick tests or small programs that you do not need to save or reuse. We can start here.

To produce our first line of code, we will use our first Python command: `print()` beside the `>>>` prompt. When you type the `print()` command, notice that the type turns color (purple). This indicates that `print()` is a command that is known to Python. In this case, Python knows to display whatever we put between the parentheses.

BTW

`print()` and other words that turn color in an IDE are considered to be reserved words in a programming language. These are available to programmers to use in the way they are predefined by the programming language. We cannot use them for any other purpose or for variable or procedure names. More about these coming up!

PROBLEM-SOLVING

► If your `print()` command is not in color, check to be sure you typed it in correctly, using all lowercase letters and that you used parentheses rather than braces or brackets.

► If you want to retrieve your previous command from the shell rather than retyping it, use *alt + p*. You can then correct or simply rerun that line of code by pressing *Enter*.

Now, we tell Python the text that we want to display inside the parentheses. We have to use quotation marks to tell Python that it should print out exactly what is between them. Python allows the use of single quotation marks or double quotation marks. However, you have to be consistent and use the same style for the opening and closing quotation marks.

Correct: `'text'` and `"text"`
Incorrect: `'text"` and `"text'`

Here is our first command in Python:

```
print("Hello, world")
```

If we use single quotes around our text field, the output will be exactly the same as using double quotes. Notice that the text inside the quotation marks turns color. This tells us that Python recognizes it as text. The Python IDLE uses green, while some online IDEs use different colors, such as red. As long as it turns a color, then Python recognizes it as text. Try both!

```
print('Hello, world')
```

produces the same output as:

```
print("Hello, world")
```

We have written our first program! It will be translated into binary code so it can be run and understood by the computer. Congratulations!

Saving Our Program

Since we typed our "Hello, world" code in the Python shell, we cannot save it. Let's learn where to place our code so we can save it and then reuse it. Saved programs in Python are also called **scripts**. Code that will be saved and rerun multiple times should use a script. A new script is created in the Python IDLE by going to *File>New File*.

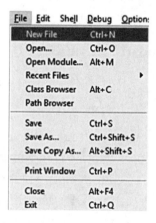

    A new window pops open. It is labeled *untitled* until we save it with a new name. Just as we did earlier, type in `print("Hello, world")` on the first blank line and press the *Enter* key. When we were in the Python shell with the `>>>` prompt, when we hit *Enter*, our print command was executed. This time, nothing happens! We have to tell Python that we are ready to execute our code. To do this using the IDLE, select "Run" from the top menu and "Run Module" from the drop-down menu that is displayed next. You can also use the "F5" function key as a shortcut to run your script.

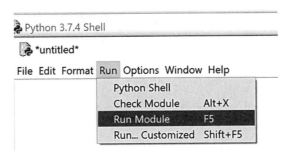

Notice that the Python IDLE makes us save our code before it will run. I recommend you create a folder for all of your programs and save it there.

If you are using the Python IDLE, your program will automatically save with the .py file extension. This is important so the IDLE will recognize the file as Python and will recognize the reserved words indicated by their colors. Once you have saved the code, it will continue executing it.

To run the program in an online editor, find and press the play button seen in most online IDEs:

▶

When using the downloaded Python IDLE, the output of your code will be displayed in the Python shell. You will see ===== **RESTART:** each time you run your code and then any output from your program. In our example, the output is:

```
=====RESTART: filename location which will be different for everyone
Hello, world
>>>
```

Congratulations again! Now you have written your first saved program in Python.

Comments

Comments document our code. It may seem unnecessary now, but if you come back to a program you wrote even just a few months (or even weeks) earlier, you will have trouble remembering the details of what you did and how you did it. Comments also make it much easier for someone else to understand what the program is doing. If you are the one who has to modify someone else's code to either correct an error or update the program, well written comments help reduce the amount of time it takes to understand the code. They can also help with correcting errors in your code. More about that in Chapter 7.

Comments are single or several lines that describe what is going on in a program. Each programming language has its own way to indicate a line of code is a comment. Comments are for people! The compiler or interpreter ignores them.

```
# The hashtag symbol starts a comment.


"""
This creates a block of comments in Python.
You must have the triple quotation marks around
    the block of comments.
"""
```

```
'''
Single quotation marks are also valid in Python
   to indicate several lines of comments.
'''
```

At the top of your program, good programming practice dictates that you should include a section of comments with the author of the program, date, and a brief description of the program's purpose.

```
# author: your name
# date created: mm/dd/yy
# date revised: mm/dd/yy
# brief description of the program's purpose
```

You should also comment sections of code that are key to the program or particularly complex. This helps you when you come back to a program as well as anyone looking at it for the first time.

REVIEW QUESTIONS

1. What does IDE or IDLE stand for?

2. What does an IDE do?

3. What command is used in Python to display text?

4. How do we tell Python what to display?

5. How are reserved words displayed in Python?

6. Is it acceptable to mix single and double quotation marks?

7. How can you tell if you are in the Python shell?

8. What file extension do Python files use?

9. What are Python programs also called?

10. Write the code to display your name.

11. Write the code to display the name of your pet or the name you would give a pet if you do not have one.

12. Give two reasons comments are used in programs.

13. What symbol is used for a single line comment in Python?

14. How do you comment several lines at once?

15. Write a block of comments to explain a program that turns on the coffee pot at different times based on whether it is a weekend day or workday.

Debugging and Testing

MUST KNOW

⚡ Bugs are errors in our program code.

⚡ Debugging is identifying and correcting our programming errors.

⚡ Syntax errors prevent the program from running until corrected.

⚡ Logic errors are a result of problems that do not prevent the program from running but do produce inaccurate results.

⚡ Runtime errors occur when certain code is executed, such as when a divide-by-zero situation occurs. It may not happen each time the code runs.

⚡ Testing our code is of critical importance. We should always test thoroughly with both valid and invalid data to ensure our program handles all possibilities properly.

e will all eventually have one or more errors in our code. Identifying and removing programming errors takes time, so it is important to develop a solid problem-solving process.

When you were typing "Hello, world" with the `print()` command, you may have received an error. I often make typing errors, and fortunately the interpreter will find them for me when it tries to run my code. Below is an error where I misspelled the word "print." I typed `"prnt"`, leaving out the letter "i" by accident. Python gives us a lot of helpful information in the error message.

```
prnt("Hello, world")

Traceback (most recent call last):
  File "<pyshell#0>", line 1, in <module>
    prnt("Hello World!")
NameError: name 'prnt' is not defined
```

Let's look at each of the lines in the error message.:

- Line 1   A "Traceback" is simply tracing or tracking to where the issue occurred.

- Line 2   This tells us the filename where the error occurred and the line number in the file.

    I wrote this line of code in the shell, so the name `<pyshell#0>` is given.

    The #0 is the first use of the shell after opening it. It resets to 0 each time you close and reopen the shell.

- Line 3   This is the actual line of code where the error occurred.

- Line 4   "NameError:" This tells us the type of error, and what "name" is in error. In our example, it accurately tells us `'prnt'` is not defined. Fortunately, this one is easy to fix!

In programming, we often refer to errors in our code as **bugs**.

IRL   "Bug" is generally accredited to a moth found by naval officer and future admiral Grace Murray Hopper in a relay of the Harvard Mark II back in 1945. She taped the moth into the logbook, which can be found in the Smithsonian Institution's National Museum of American History. While the term "bug" had been used earlier than this, this was the first time an *actual insect* was found. The term stuck and is still used today.

Testing your program code is another step in the iterative development process discussed in Chapter 3. It is critical to do a thorough job of testing before releasing your program to others to use. Sometimes, our fingers do not type what our brain told us to type. You do not expect an error, but, alas, you have one.

Remember with the iterative development process, we break down, or decompose, our algorithms until we get to programmable sections of code. We code a section, test it, and then correct any errors. We then test again and correct any errors. We test again until all errors that we can find are identified and corrected. We now have a working chunk of code that we should not have to worry about again. We can move on to write another block of code. As we get multiple blocks, we must be sure to include testing of the connections between the working blocks.

There are three general categories of errors.

- **Syntax**   These are like grammar errors in our code. Programming languages have their own syntax based on the punctuation and rules for using them. Typos fall into this category along with mismatched parentheses and braces and needed punctuation.

  Syntax errors are found when the compiler or interpreter are converting our code to machine code. Our code will not compile correctly until we find and correct our syntax errors. Most compilers and interpreters will provide a line number where the error was found and a description of the error to help the programmer with finding it. Sometimes, the error messages are not helpful! For example, in the line of code below, I forgot the closing parenthesis. The error message

I received is a little confusing. EOF stands for "End Of File" and parsing means the Python interpreter was working on my line of code to break it into smaller elements to translate it to machine code.

```
print ("Hello, world"
```

- **Logic** These errors do not cause compile time or interpreter errors and may not be found until the program runs. Logic errors could be the result of using an addition sign + rather than a subtraction sign – in a calculation or using the wrong value. It may not be found unless the programmer does detailed testing to compare actual results to expected results. In the line of code below, I am subtracting 2 rather than adding 2 to the score. Oops! This is a logic error. There is nothing wrong with using subtraction on this line of code. It is up to me as the programmer to realize the score is incorrect through testing and to correct my code.

```
score = score - 2
```

- **Runtime** Runtime errors occur when the program is executing. The program compiles with no syntax errors. An example of this could be an occurrence that results in a "divide-by-0" situation. The program could run successfully many times, never encountering zero as the divisor. However, the program will end with an error if and when a zero does occur. In the example below, I am calculating some stats for a game, but my divisor, score, is 0 for this execution of the program.

As you can see, I get a `ZeroDivisionError: division by zero` error. Anytime score is not 0, the program will run successfully, but as soon as it is zero, this error will occur.

```
>>> score = 0
>>> numGames = 5
>>> stats = numGames / score
Traceback (most recent call last):
  File "<pyshell#2>", line 1, in <module>
    stats = numGames / score
ZeroDivisionError: division by zero
>>>
```

Testing

I cannot tell you how many times students turned in programming assignments that would not run due to syntax errors! That tells me they never even ran the program themselves to see if it worked. While I applaud their confidence, I was not happy with their lack of testing.

We all make mistakes with our code. Even with simple programs, we can easily have a typo. Get in the habit of doing a good job testing your code!

- **Good testing habits**   Always run your code to ensure there are no syntax errors.

    Prepare expected results to compare against actual results to ensure there are no logic errors. This means select data to use and determine the output that should occur before you run the program. Then run the program to see if it does produce the expected output.

    Think of all the possible ways someone could use your program.

■ **Test "boundary" conditions** If your code is checking for values less than 100, then be sure to test 100 and also the "boundary" conditions of 99 and 101. *Off-by-one* errors frequently occur.

IRL When I worked for a major soft drink company, I remember a time when my project manager was giving a demonstration of our code to our user community. Everything worked perfectly, because the project manager knew how it was supposed to work. However, the users then started to test it out. They used it in combinations that were not expected and errors started showing up right and left! While it was embarrassing, our software project ended up being much better as a result—after the errors were fixed, of course!

■ **Invalid data** Always be sure to test your software with invalid data. As an example, if you are asking the user to enter a number, be sure to test with a letter or special character, and vice versa.

Comment-out sections of code to help identify where an error is occurring. Commenting out working code in longer programs also helps your testing go faster. You can skip earlier sections of a program and get to the part where you think the issue is occurring.

Use the `print()` statement to display intermediate results of variables or to see if your program reaches a certain line of code before the error occurs. I often use `print("Got here")` when I am trying to find the cause of an error.

Remember that your name is associated with the program, so if there are errors that you did not find, it is your reputation that will be impacted!

REVIEW QUESTIONS

1. What is debugging?

2. Why should we test our program with invalid data?

3. What is a boundary value?

4. What is an expected result?

5. If you are writing a program to convert temperatures from Fahrenheit to Celsius, list at least three tests you should run on the code.

6. What type of error occurs if a program tries to add a number to a text field?

7. What error type occurs if a reserved word is misspelled? Example: `prnt()`.

8. What type of error occurs if I am dividing and mix up the dividend and divisor?

9. What errors are in the following lines of code:
   a. `Print("Let's go team!")`
   b. `print('Time to level up")`
   c. `print{"What time is it?"}`

Flashcard App

 # Variables and Assignment Statements

MUST⚡KNOW

⚡ Variables hold values in a program.

⚡ Programmers determine variable names in the program.

⚡ There are syntax rules to follow for naming variables.

⚡ Assignment statements are used to assign a value to a variable.

⚡ Programming languages evaluate what is on the right-hand side of the equal sign and assign it to the variable on the left-hand side of the equal sign.

We are ready to start writing code that is more complex than our simple `"Hello, world"` program. Our first new concept is a **variable**, which is simply a holding place for a value.

The programmer decides what to name variables used in a program. Each programming language has its own rules for naming variables. The following rules and conventions are common across many programming languages.

- **Rule 1**   A variable should start with a letter, usually lowercase.

  Some languages allow an underscore **_** to be used to start a variable name.

  Numbers can be used in variable names, but not as the first character:

  `student1`

- **Rule 2**   No spaces between letters. While a space is a valid character, it is not valid in a variable name.

  If a space is used, then the programming language thinks it is seeing two separate variable names.

  `firstName` → valid variable name.
  `first name` → not valid. Programming languages will think there are two variables because of the space.

- **Rule 3**   No special characters. Most programming languages do not allow special characters, such as @, #, !, $, %, &, *, to be used in a variable name. As mentioned above, the underscore is usually acceptable.

  `_name` → OK
  `name!` → not OK

- **Rule 4**   Upper- and lowercase letters matter. Variable names are case sensitive. The following names are all different variable names:

  `age`
  `Age`
  `AGE`
  `aGe`

- **Rule 5** No reserved words. Each programming language has its list of reserved words. These show up in color in most programming environments to help identify them. These are already known to the language and have special functionality associated with them. You cannot use reserved words as variable names.

- **Convention 1** Use "camelCase" when combining words for your variable names. camelCase occurs when the first character of the second word (and any subsequent ones) is capitalized. This makes it much easier for our brains to process and recognize the variable name.

  `testScore` is easier to read than `testscore`.

- **Convention 2** Use descriptive names. If you use variable names that describe the data they hold, then the program code is much easier to understand. For example, if I am writing a program to track student names, then a variable:

  `stuName` is much clearer than `sn`.

Assignment Statements

So, we now have variable names. Great! What can we do with them? Since we said they can hold a value, let's find out how to place a value in a variable.

Programming languages have a specific way to assign a value to a variable. We assign a value to a variable by means of an Assignment Statement. Most of them will use a single equals sign `=` to do this.

`age = 16` assigns the number 16 to the variable `age`
`day = 25` assigns the number 25 to the variable `day`

We can use our `print()` command to print the value a variable contains. The number 16 will be displayed in the example below.

```
age = 16
print(age)

# The output below is displayed:
===== RESTART:
16
>>>
```

It is important to understand that programming languages evaluate what is on the right-hand side of the equals sign and assign the outcome to the variable on the left-hand side of the equals sign.

A useful thing you can do with variables is change their value. What?!

age = 21   This sets the value of **age** to be 21. The former value of 16 is gone and forgotten!

You can also use an expression to evaluate and assign the answer to a variable.

age = 16 + 1   The right side is processed: 16 + 1 and the sum, which is 17, is assigned to the variable **age**.

print(age)   displays 17

You can use another variable in part of the expression.

yearsToVote = 21 − age   Notice the use of **camelCase** with the variable name!

print(yearsToVote)   Our **age** variable was set to 17 in the example above.
The expression *21 minus* **age** will be evaluated: 21 − 17.
The value 4 will be displayed.

Similarly, two variables can be used for our calculation.

`age = 15` The variable `age` is now set to the value 15.

`votingAge = 21` The variable `votingAge` is set to the value 21.

`yearsToVote = votingAge — age`

> The right-hand side of the equals sign is evaluated:
>
> > `votingAge — age` which is 21 − 15 is calculated and assigned to the variable `yearsToVote`.

`print(yearsToVote)` The value 6 is displayed by the `print()` statement.

More complicated expressions can be used.

`celsius = 22` The temperature in Celsius is set to 22.

`fahrenheit = ((9 * celsius) / 5) + 32`

> The expression to convert Celsius to fahrenheit is evaluated. The result is then stored in the variable `fahrenheit`.

You can also use an expression in a `print()` statement that will be evaluated and then the results printed.

`print((9 * celsius) / 5 + 32)`

> This statement will calculate and print the result but the calculated value is not stored in a variable.

BTW

In math class, you would write the equation to convert Celsius to Fahrenheit something like "Fahrenheit = Celsius(9/5) + 32."

In programming, however, you have to include all of the math symbols or you will receive a syntax error. We'll look at math symbols in more detail in Chapter 10.

Variables in Assignment Statements

In the last section, we introduced assignment statements to give variables a value. Another way of using a variable is to use it on the right- *and* left-hand sides of the equals sign.

```
score = score + 2
```

Remember the right-hand side of the assignment statement is evaluated, and then the result is stored in the variable on the left-hand side of the equals sign. You can take the current value of a variable, change it in some way, and then store the new value back into the variable overwriting the former value. This concept is often a little confusing for new programmers.

The example below takes the current value of score, which is 42, adds 2 to the value, and then assigns the new number back in score, overwriting the former value of 42.

`score = 42`	Assign the value 42 to the variable `score`.
`score = score + 2`	Add 2 to the current value of `score`: $42 + 2$. Store the value 44 back in `score` overwriting the previous value.

```
print ("The current score is:", score)
```

This code will display:

```
The current score is: 44
```

So, variables are holding places for values. There are rules for naming variables and for using them in programming statements. We can calculate or assign a value to a variable and then use the variable as many times as our program needs without having to recalculate its value. This makes our programs more efficient.

More Printing Options

The `print()` command can print more than one thing at a time. It's easier to understand if a message states what the value being printed is rather than just the number. In the earlier example, it would be better to state the number is an age. We could code:

```
print("Age: ", age)
```

We could also include more text fields and variables in a `print()` statement. Each one must be separated by a comma. If we had more data about a user, such as address and telephone number, we can include all of this in a `print()` statement. Remember text fields have quotation marks around them. The `print()` statement will display exactly what is within the quotation marks.

```
print("Age: ", age, "Address: ", address, "Tele-
    phone number: ", phoneNum)
```

In the above case all of the information prints on one line, which may be fine at times.

```
Age: 17 Address: 1600 Pennsylvania Avenue Phone
    Number: 123-456-7890
```

The output could look better though. This is where *escape characters* can come in handy. These are formating instructions to Python that are used inside a text field to be printed. Escape characters start with a backslash character "\". Do not confuse this with the forward slash "/". The backslash is found above the *Enter* key on many keyboards. The **"\"** tells the `print()` command to treat the character after the backslash differently.

`\n`	Go to a new line, then continue printing.
`\t`	Add spacing for a tab, then continue printing.
`\"`	Print the quotation marks rather than considering them the end of the text field.
`\'`	Print the single quotation mark rather than considering it the end of the text field.
`\\`	Print a backslash character.

There are other escape characters, but these take care of a lot of formating needs. Check the official Python documentation to see the others.

Here is an example of our above `print()` statement using escape characters to print each value on a new line and to indent the second and third lines one tab level.

```
print("Age: ", age, "\n\tAddress: ", address,
  "\n\tTelephone number: ", phoneNum)
```

Our output with the formatting included looks like this:

```
Age: 17
  Address: 1600 Pennsylvania Avenue
  Phone Number: 123-456-7890
```

There are other formatting tools in Python. When you want to include a comma to separate the thousands in a number, you can use a special text formatting tool:

```
"{:,}".format(number to format)
```

For example, if we have a variable with a large value and want to print it with commas, we use:

```
number = 1234567890
print("{:,}".format(number))
```

Our output is:

```
1,234,567,890
```

Note that the formatting tool also works with single quotation marks.

```
print('{:,} '.format(number))
```

As you might guess, there are other ways to do commonly needed formatting.

To indicate the number of decimal places to print, we can use `{:.2f}`, where 2 is the number of decimals to print and can be changed for your needs. To print the value of pi to 4 decimal places, we could use:

```
pi = 3.14159265
print("The value of Pi is: {:.4f} ".format(pi))
```

And the output is:

```
The value of Pi is: 3.1416
```

If you are working with percentages and want to add the % symbol, insert it in place of the *f* in the above print statement.

```
print("The percentage is: {:.3%} ".format(pi))
```

This will output:

```
The percentage is: 314.159%
```

Notice that Python took our value of pi and shifted the fields so we printed three decimal places rather than the eight the variable has.

None of these formatting tools change the value of our variable. They only change how the output will be displayed.

While these formatting options will take care of most of your needs, there are more formatting options in the official Python documentation.

REVIEW QUESTIONS

1. Are the following valid variable names? If not, what rule is broken?
    a. `carTag`
    b. `OptioN`
    c. `locker#`
    d. `alarm time`

2. Is `asdf` a good variable name? Why or why not?

3. What variable name would you use to represent your favorite snack?

4. What variable name would you use to represent the music you listen to most often?

5. What variable name would you use to represent the location you receive mail?

6. What is the symbol used for assignment statements?

7. Can you change the value of a variable once it has been assigned a value?

8. Can a variable be used to calculate the value of a different variable?

9. How would you code the assignment statement for a variable to hold the number of games your favorite sports team plays this season?

10. How would you code the assignment statement for a variable to hold the calculation of the winning percentage of a team (wins/losses)?

11. How would you code the assignment statement for a variable to hold the calculation of the average number of days in your Snapchat streaks?

12. What is printed in this example?
```
testScore = 92
extraCredit = 5
testScore = testScore + extraCredit
print(testScore)
```

13. You are setting up a gaming tournament. Every time a new registration comes in, add one to the variable `numberOfPlayers`.

14. Each time a registered player checks in for the tournament, subtract one from the number of `noShows`.

15. Using only one `print()` statement with escape characters, print the total number of registrations on one line and the `numberofPlayers` on the second line, indented one level, and the number of `noShows` on the third line, also indented one level.

16. Our tournament is huge with many players registered to attend. Set up a formatted print statement to use commas to separate the number of registered players, number of players, and number of no shows.

17. We have three test scores that we want to average. Calculate and print the average with three decimal places.

Data Types

MUST ⚡ KNOW

⚡ Variables have a data type.

⚡ The basic variable types are `int`, `float`, and `str`.

⚡ You can change a variable's data type using casting.

⚡ A character in a text field must look like a number to successfully convert.

⚡ Casting from `floats` (decimal numbers) to `ints` (integers) results in the truncation of decimal values.

A program can process several kinds of data and each data element has a **type**. This means we can define our variables to hold numbers or letters. There are two basic types of numbers: integers and real numbers. It is important to make the distinction because programming languages store these numbers in memory differently.

Python is much more forgiving than many languages. If you declare a variable and assign it a value, Python determines the data type based on the value you assign it.

`age = 18` This creates a variable that will be an `integer` data type.

`avg = 4.5` This creates a variable that will be a real number meaning the variable has a decimal point. Its data type is `float`, for floating-point decimal.

`name = "me"` This creates a variable that holds text and will be a `string` data type.

BTW

"Whole number" and "integer" refer to the same type of number, which is one without a decimal. A real number is one with a decimal, even if the value after the decimal is 0.

BTW

There are other numeric data types with specific uses, but many programs can be successfully written with just `ints` and `floats`

 IRL   **Many other programming languages require variables to be defined with an assigned data type before using it in the program.**

Numbers that have the `float` data type are stored imprecisely in computer memory in all programming languages. For example, 1.5 could be stored as 1.4999999.

Integers are stored exactly as their value represents. 5 is stored in memory as 5.

Internally, the programming language makes the adjustments for the imprecision of floats, but because of this inexactness, programmers should use integers with money calculations, then convert it to a decimal number to avoid potential rounding errors. Python has other built-in modules such as *Decimal* and *Fraction* to use with real numbers. See the official Python documentation for more detail if you need these.

If you try to store a decimal value in an `int` (integer) variable, you will get an error in some languages, such as Java. Python, being flexible, will dynamically convert the variable from an `int` to a `float` data type, which can hold decimals.

Text fields are called `strings` in many programming languages, including Python and Java. To indicate that a value is a text field, or string, quotation marks must be around the value. We did this with our first program where we printed `"Hello, world"`. Anything inside the quotation marks is mirrored exactly as it is when the output is displayed.

Python can start using a variable as soon as it is created and assigned a value, and it will take on the data type of the initial value. Since most programming languages require variables to be "declared" or "defined" before they can be used, it is a good idea to get in the habit of declaring your variables and assigning them an initial value at the top of your program, after your comments.

BTW

A common error that new programmers make is to use a variable for the first time in an assignment statement: `score = score + 6` This will result in an error, because the variable `score` will not have a value until the assignment statement is completed. Remember the right-hand side of the equal sign is processed and then assigned to the variable on the left-hand side of the equal sign. When `score` is referenced on the right-hand side of the assignment statement, it does not exist yet, and the following error will occur:

`NameError: name 'score' is not defined`

```
# declare variables
firstName = ""  # This will create a string data
                # type with no value
lastName = ""
age = 0
testAvg = 0.0
```

In Python, `None` is a data type, not a value. `None` is used to indicate a variable exists, but it does not have a value yet. It is similar to a null value in other programming languages. A variable can be set to a value of and tested for a value of `None`:

```
smallestNum = None
```

Converting Data Types, or "Casting"

There are times in programming when you need to change a data type. This happens often in Python when prompting a user to input data from the keyboard. In Python, the data *always* comes into the program from the keyboard as a `string` data type. Even if you are asking for a number, it starts out as a string. (We'll talk more about this is in Chapter 12.)

As long as what the user types in looks like a number, it can be converted to an integer or float. This is called **casting**. We are casting, or changing the value to be a new data type.

In this example, we have a variable named `value`. It initially holds a string value of `"12345"`. Since this is in quotation marks, it is a text field and we cannot perform math operations, such as addition or division, on a string field.

```
value = "12345"
```

We can convert it to be an integer or a decimal number by using a built-in function. Built-in functions are prewritten and tested code that are included with the programming language. We have already used one, the `print()` function. These also change color when using the Python IDLE, so we realize that it already has a designated purpose in Python.

The built-in function to convert a string to an integer is `int()`.

```
value = int(value)
```

This takes the current contents of our variable and converts it to be an integer and stores it back in the same variable. Since the text field contents look like numbers, our casting conversion is successful. Python also updates the data type to be an integer.

We can also convert a float or decimal number to be an integer using the same `int()` function.

Truncation means the decimal point and anything after it are sliced off. There is no rounding up or down. Everything is simply lopped off from the decimal point and all numbers to the right of it.

```
decimal = 5.5
num1 = int(decimal)
```
Notice we stored our converted value in a different variable.

```
print(decimal)
5.5
```
This shows the contents of the variable decimal are unchanged.

```
print(num1)
5
```
This shows our value was truncated when converted to an integer.

The built-in function to convert a string to a float data type is `float()`. Surprised, aren't you.

```
value = "123.45"
value = float(value)
```

This takes the current contents of our variable and converts it to a real number. We store the new contents with the new data type back in our same variable. The variable, value, now holds the number 123.45. Since the text field contents look like numbers, our casting conversion is successful.

```
print(value)
123.45
```
This shows our variable was converted to a decimal number.

If you try to convert a string value that does not "look" like a number to an **int** or **float**, you will receive an error message.

```
weather = "hot"
weather = int(weather)
```
The following error message occurs since **"hot"** is not comprised of characters that look like numbers.

```
Traceback (most recent call last):
  File "<pyshell#1>", line 1, in <module>
    weather = int(weather)
ValueError: invalid literal for int() with base
  10: 'hot'
>>>
```

You can also convert **ints** and **floats** to be **strings**. Math operations cannot be performed on the variable after the conversion.

```
phoneNumber = 1234567890
phoneNumber = str(phoneNumber)
```
This converts the data to be a string data type.

```
temperature = 87.6
outsideTemp = str(temperature)
```

How to Verify a Data Type

In Python, the `type()` built-in function can show you the data type of a variable. While you may not use it in a final version of a program, it can help with troubleshooting errors in your code. Sometimes, you may have a field that is the wrong data type, which could cause errors or skew the expected results. Printing the data type of the variables in use could help identify the error.

```
userData = "5"
print(type(userData))
<class 'str'>
```
The data type for the variable `userData` is `string`.

```
userData = int(userData)
```
Casts the data type to be an integer.

```
print(type(userData))
<class 'int'>
```
The data type is now `int` for integer.

In this chapter, we've covered the concepts of data type for our variables. These data types can be numbers or text fields. The basic number data types are `int` and `float` while text fields are `str`.

REVIEW QUESTIONS

1. Which data type allows decimals?

2. Which of the following values are data type `int`?

    ```
    0, 42.0, -999, 14.4, 11.0
    ```

3. What are text fields called in Python?

4. How do programmers tell Python a field is a text field?

5. Which of the following values are valid floating-point numbers?

    ```
    -0.5, -1.0, 0.0, 5, 92, 5432.1
    ```

6. Define a variable called `pet` and initialize it to the type of pet, such as dog, that you have or would like to have.

7. Define and initialize a variable and assign it your first name.

8. What happens when we cast a `float()` data type to be an `int()` data type?

9. Will the following code cause an error?

    ```
    address = "440"
    addressF = float(address)
    ```

10. Will the following code cause an error?

    ```
    addrGov = "1600 Pennsylvania Avenue"
    addrGov = int(addrGov)
    ```

11. Create a variable to hold your most recent locker number.
    Convert it to be a `string` field.
    Print your variable.

12. What does truncate mean?

13. When could truncation occur with Python data types?

14. What command is used to determine the data type of a variable?

15. Define a variable to count the number of times you throw a tennis ball to your dog.

> Set it to an initial value.
> Print the variable.
> Print the data type of the variable.

Use the code below for the next three questions.

```
age = "18"
age = float(age)
age = int(age)
```

16. What will be the data type of the variable age after line 1?

17. What will be the data type of the variable age after line 2?

18. What will be the data type of the variable age after line 3?

10 Math Symbols

MUST KNOW

⚡ The standard math operations are available in programming languages.

⚡ The symbols are the same as are used in math, except for multiplication.

⚡ The output of modulus math is the remainder of two numbers after dividing.

⚡ The order of operations for mathematics and programming is the same.

e have already used a little bit of math in some of our calculations. Fortunately, since the standard math symbols are used in programming, you were able to easily understand the expression to be calculated. As noted earlier, you have to specify each math operation. You cannot write 2(x + 5) or you will get a syntax error. You must write: $2 * (x + 5)$.

Mathematical Operations

The most popular programming languages share the same symbols for the most common math operations:

Addition	+	
Subtraction	−	
Multiplication	*	This is the asterisk, which is above the number 8 key on most keyboards.
Division	/	
Exponent	**	

Division with whole numbers or integers is handled differently with different programming languages. Many of them, including Java and Python version 2, will truncate the decimal portion of division *only* when both the dividend and divisor are integers. Watch for this in other programming languages.

BTW

Watch the direction of the division symbol. There is another keyboard key that goes in the other direction \. The backward slash is not used for division, and you will have a syntax error.

```
print(5/2)
```
will print 2 — Java and Python2 produce this result because two integers are being divided.

```
print(5.0 / 2)
```
will print 2.5 — The numerator has a decimal so truncation does *not* occur with either Python 2 or 3.

`print(5 / 2.0)`   will print 2.5   The denominator has a decimal so truncation does *not* occur with either Python 2 or 3.

Python version 3, which this book uses, does maintain the decimal portion of the answer with division when using two integers.

`print(5 / 2)`   will print 2.5

However, note that when a value is cast as an integer, the decimal portion is truncated. See the previous chapter on casting for more information.

`print(int(5 / 2))`   will print 2 in Python3 as well as Java.

Modulus Math

Modulus math, also called **modulo math**, or mod math, uses division but only provides the *remainder*, not the quotient. While modulus math is not used often in high school math classes, it has several common uses in programming.

`Modulus    %`	The percent sign is used for modulus math in Python.
	Some programming languages use the word MOD for modulus math.
`20 % 5 = 0`	The quotient is 4 with a *remainder* of 0.
`21 % 5 = 1`	The quotient is 4 with a *remainder* of 1.
`3 % 5 = 3`	Anytime the first number is smaller than the second, the *remainder* will always be the first number.

A common use for "mod math" is to find even or odd numbers. A number that is divisible by 2 with a remainder of 0 is even.

`num % 2 = 0`

Order of Operations

The order of operations applies in programming exactly as it does in math. **PEMDAS** is a commonly used mnemonic to help us remember the order of operations. PEMDAS stands for "Please Excuse My Dear Aunt Sally" and provides the order to process the operations when it is not explicitly indicated by using parentheses.

> P = parentheses
>
> E = exponents
>
> M = multiplication
>
> D = division

Multiplication and division are interchangeable. Whichever comes first from the left to right will be evaluated first.

> A = addition
>
> S = subtraction

Addition and subtraction are interchangeable. Whichever occurs first from left to right will be evaluated first.

```
num1 = 14 + 15 + 16 * 2 / 5      num1 would equal 35.4
num2 = (14 + 15 + 16) * 2 / 5    num2 would equal 18.0
```

Performing mathematical operations in programming is exactly the same as solving them by hand in your math class. The order of operations determines how to evaluate an expression. It is always a good idea to use parentheses to indicate your intent with a multistep calculation. It will make your code easier to read and understand for someone else.

REVIEW QUESTIONS

1. What are the symbols used for math operations in programming languages?

2. When does truncation occur with some programming languages, such as Python 2 or Java?

3. Write the code to calculate the average of three test scores, and store the result in a variable.

4. Write the code to determine how many pizzas to order for 5 people assuming everyone will eat 3 slices of pizza and there are 8 slices per pizza.

5. Can the / and \ signs both be used for division?

6. What is the value of the variable `calc`?
   ```
   calc = 2**3
   ```

7. What is the symbol for modulus math in Python?

8. What is the result of modulus math?

9. What value is stored in the variable `time1`?
   ```
   hour = 7
   time1 = hour % 12
   ```

10. What value is stored in the variable `time2`?
    ```
    hour = 18
    time2 = hour % 12
    ```

11. Write the calculation to determine if a number is odd.

12. Write the code to determine if a number is divisible by 3.

13. What is the value of the variable `num`?
    ```
    num = 1.0 * (17 / 3) - 2
    ```

14. Write the code to calculate the circumference of a circle with a radius of 4 and store the result in a variable. Remember the circumference equation is: `2 * pi * r`.

15. Write the code for the following equation:

Take your shoe size, multiply it by 5. Add 50. Multiply by 20. Add 1020. Subtract the year you were born. Print the result.

Flashcard App

Strings

MUST ⚡ KNOW

⚡ Each character in a string has an index position, which is an integer showing its location in the string.

⚡ Concatenation uses the plus sign (+) and, when used with strings, will "glue" them together.

⚡ Strings are immutable, meaning they cannot be changed.

⚡ "Slicing" a string means taking a selection of it. The format is: *variable* [start:stop], where the value of *start* is included and the value of *stop* is *not* included.

⚡ In Python, strings can be compared using the same relational operators used with numbers: >, >=, <, <=, ==, and !=.

he string data type gets its own chapter since we often need to work with text fields in our programs. There are several ways strings are frequently processed, and this chapter covers those. A variable can hold one string, even though the string could consist of several words and symbols. Whatever characters are included between the set of quotation marks is considered one **string**. Remember that either single or double quotation marks can be used as long as you are consistent. Most programming languages only use double quotation marks, so it's a good idea for you to do the same.

Index and Length

Even though there are often multiple symbols in a string, we sometimes need to get to individual characters. Each character has a position in the string. The position is represented by an integer and is called an **index value**. Python, as well as many other programming languages, start counting the first index position with 0. Odd, isn't it? If we have a variable with the string value "programming", the letter *p* is at index position 0. The letter *o* is at index position 2.

course = "programming"

String characters	p	r	o	g	r	a	m	m	i	n	g
index position	0	1	2	3	4	5	6	7	8	9	10

Notice that the index positions go from 0 to 10, which are eleven positions.

To access an individual character in a string, Python uses square brackets with the needed index position inside the brackets.

`course[1]`　　The character at index position 1 is *r*.

`course[5]`　　The character at index position 5 is *a*.

There is a built-in length function, `len()` in Python, that we can use to determine the **length** of a string. You provide the name of a variable or a string in the parentheses. The function `len()` then returns how many characters are stored in the variable or are in the string.

`print(len(course))`   This prints the number of characters stored in the variable *course*.

`11`   There are 11 characters in the string "programming".

The last character of the string can also be referenced using the index position `(len(string) − 1)`. You do not have to know how many characters there are. You can just use:

`course[len(course) − 1]` to access the last character, which is *g* in our example.

This looks confusing, so let's break it down.

1. Our variable is `course`.

2. The `len()` built-in function requires an argument to determine the length, so we place our variable name, `course`, inside the parentheses.

3. We want the last index position in our variable. To avoid manually counting how many characters there are, we can use the length minus 1: `len(course) −1`. This is because the index positions start at 0 and end at one less than the length.

Notice in the above example that we calculated the index position using subtraction. We can calculate the index position in any number of ways.

`course[7−4]`   This value is index 3, which holds the character *o*.

`position = 8`	This defines a variable and assigns it the value 8.
`course[1 + position]`	This index value is 9, which holds the character *n*.
`Course[2**3]`	This uses exponents, 2^3, which is $2 * 2 * 2 = 8$. The character at index 8 is *i*.

Now we have to be careful when we select or calculate an index. If we provide a number that is too large for our string, then we will receive an error.

`course[44]`	Our string only has index positions 0–10.

This will cause the following error message to display:

```
Traceback (most recent call last):
  File "<pyshell#52>", line 1, in <module>
    course[44]
IndexError: string index out of range
```

The last line of the error message tells us that the index was out of range. You might be surprised to find that the following does *not* produce an error.

`course[-1]`

It actually tells Python to start at the last index position.

`print(course[-1])`	
g	Prints the character at the last index position, or (length –1).
`print(course[-10])`	
r	Prints the character at index position 1, (length – 10).

Note that we can get an `IndexError: string index out of range` error if we use a negative number that would calculate a value outside of our indices.

```
course[-22]
```

This would calculate to (length – 22), or 11 – 22 = –11, which is an invalid index.

```
Traceback (most recent call last):
    File "<pyshell#58>", line 1, in <module>
        course[-22]
IndexError: string index out of range
```

Concatenation

We use quotation marks around the letters, symbols, numbers, or words to let the programming language know these should be considered text fields. Even if a string contains numbers, it is considered to be a text field, and mathematical operations, such as addition and division, cannot be performed. However, strings do have their own version of "math" called **concatenation**. When you use the plus sign, +, with strings, Python will concatenate, or glue the strings together.

```
cheer1 = "Let's go "
```
Notice the space after *go*.

```
cheer2 = "team!"
```
We could have placed a space before *team!*

```
cheer3 = cheer1 + cheer2
print(cheer3)
```

This will display:

Let's go team!

Python is smart enough to know that the plus sign means addition when the data types are numbers, either integers or floats (numbers with decimals), and to use concatenation when the data types are strings. The + method is overloaded, meaning there is more than one way to use it in our code. The method used is based on the data types using it. It uses addition with numbers and concatenation with strings.

However, if you use the plus sign, +, with a string and a number field, you will receive an error.

```
address = "440"
address = address + 1            Attempt to add 1 to 440


Traceback (most recent call last):
  File "<pyshell#65>", line 1, in <module>
    address = address + 1
TypeError: Can't convert 'int' object to str
implicitly
```

You can also use the multiplication sign, *, with strings. Again, Python is smart enough to recognize that with strings, this operator * means to duplicate them the number of times indicated. * is also overloaded and uses the correct version based on the data type of the values using it: numbers are multiplied and strings are repeated.

```
print(cheer3 * 3)
```
will produce:

Let's go team!Let's go team!Let's go team!

We can even use the multiplication sign with strings to store the new value, not just print it.

```
cheer3 = cheer3 * 2
print(cheer3)
```

Let's go team!Let's go team!

```
address = "440"
address = address * 5
print(address)
440440440440440
```

Note that subtraction, −, and division, /, do not have equivalent functions with strings.

Immutable

Immutable is a word that means unchangeable. Many programming languages do not allow changes to be made to a string. In Python, if you try to change a character in a string:

```
fruit = "Apple"
fruit[0] = "a"
```
Attempts to change the first character to lowercase.

You will get an error message.

```
Traceback (most recent call last):
  File "<pyshell#2>", line 1, in <module>
    fruit[0] = "a"
TypeError: 'str' object does not support item
assignment
```

Notice what happens in this next case. We will create two variables and then concatenate and store the result in a third variable.

```
greet1 = "Hello, "
greet2 = "World"
```

```
greet1 = greet1 + greet2
```
Remember the plus sign, +, is used to glue strings together.

```
print(greet1)
```
We concatenate `greet1` and `greet2` and store the result in `greet1`.

```
Hello World
```
This is the output – what??? Why didn't we get an error?

What happens in this case is Python does not actually change the original string value in `greet1`. Instead, it creates a new location in memory for our concatenated string, "Hello, World", and stores that new location in `greet1`. We did not change the original! Python helped us avoid the error behind the scenes.

When you try to change a text field, programming languages return a copy of the string with the change made to it, and the original stays the same. This did not work with the first example because we were attempting to only change a character in a string. Python cannot create a new version of the string when we use the index position to change one symbol.

One way to see behind the scenes is to use the `id()` function to see the unique identifier, which is essentially the memory address assigned to a variable. Let's use it with the example above.

```
greet1 = "Hello "
```
```
print(id(greet1))
```
The value displayed will be different for each computer.

```
68922408
```
```
greet1 = "Hello, world!"
```
```
print(id(greet1))
```
The identifier for `greet1` is different.

```
18930304
```

The unique identifier changed for `greet1` when we changed our string contents. We did not change the original string itself. We assigned a new string value to the variable resulting in a new unique identifier (memory address).

Slicing

Programs often need to work with a section of a string. Python does this using a technique called **slicing**. This always makes me think of a loaf of sliced bread. The individual slices are like the symbols in our string. Slicing strings is similar to taking slices of bread from the loaf. The format in Python is:

`variable[start:stop]`

Start represents the index position to start the selection or slice. It is *inclusive*, meaning the character at that position is included in the selection.

Stop represents the index position to stop the selection or slice. It is *exclusive*, meaning the character at that position is *not* included.

`cheer = "Go team!"`

value	G	o		t	e	a	m	!
index	0	1	2	3	4	5	6	7

`print(cheer[0:2])` would print "Go".

> G is the letter at index position 0, and it is included with slicing.
>
> A blank space is at index position 2, but that one is exclusive.
>
> So, we start at index 0, include index position 1, but do not include index 2.
>
> Our result is "Go".

`print(cheer[3:6])` would print "tea".

> Index position 3 contains the letter *t*.
>
> We take the letters up to but *not* including the one at index 6.
>
> So the letters from index 3 to 5 are "tea".

If you leave the starting position blank, then the slice starts at the beginning.

`cheer[:4]` results in "Go t"

Our string slice includes the letters at indices 0, 1, 2, and 3.

If you leave the ending position blank, then the slice goes all the way to the end.

`cheer[4:]` results in "eam!"

This string begins at index 4, but *does include* the character at index position 7.

You might think the "!" would *not* be included, but this is the only format that does not exclude the character at the last index position.

Leaving both blank would select the entire text field.

`cheer[:]` results in "Go team!"

Again, note that the character stored in the last index position is included in this slice.

Even though we get an **IndexError: string index out of range** error when we use an index position that is too large, with slicing, you can reference an index position that does not exist for the string, and you will not receive an error!

With our "Go team!" string example, if we type:

`c1 = cheer[8:9]`   Note that the numbers used in our slice are out of the range of our string

If we print *c*1, then nothing is displayed on our output console.

`print(c1)`

We can get a better picture of what is going on by printing the length of our variable *c*1. We use the built-in function **len()** to see the length.

`print(len(c1))`

0   The length of our string *c*1 is 0. This is because our slice used values 8:9 that are outside of the size of our string.

The string $c1$ was created, but it is empty, and we did not get a `string index out of range` error!

Similarly, if we start our slice with a value too large for our string and do not include an ending position, we do not get an error, and the new slice is empty with a length of 0.

```
c2 = cheer[11:]
print(len(c2))
0
```

Again, if we try to reference an index position without slicing that is not in our string, then we get the `IndexError`.

```
c2 = cheer[11]
```
Note that this is not slicing. It is only referencing the character at index position 11.

```
Traceback (most recent call last):
    File "<pyshell#5>", line 1, in <module>
        c2 = cheer[11]
IndexError: string index out of range
```

It is important to recognize that a blank space is a valid character. The character at index position 2 in our string variable *cheer* example is the space. If we take a slice to only select the space at index position 2 and then test the length of it, we will see that its length is 1, not 0.

```
c3 = cheer[2:3]
print(len(c3))
1
```

String slicing has some unusual rules that you will just have to learn or look up in the official Python documentation before using in your programs.

String Comparisons

You can compare strings (text fields) using the same relational operators we used to compare numbers:

<	less than
<=	less than or equal to
>	greater than
>=	greater than or equal to
==	equal to
!=	not equal

Strings are compared using the alphabet similar to how a dictionary places words in alphabetical order. Remember that strings are case sensitive. A capital letter is different than a lowercase letter.

Comparisons are made using the ASCII table (American Standard Code for Information Interchange—just in case you really wanted to know what it stands for). It is pronounced as "æ ski." This table has a binary representation for each letter and symbol on the standard American English keyboard. It started as the ASCII table but has expanded to accommodate different languages and is called the Unicode table. The Unicode table has over 137,000 characters in it, and the first 128 characters in the table are the same as the ASCII table.

An excerpt of the table is below. The full ASCII table contains the binary, hexadecimal, and octal equivalents for every character. Since it is much easier for us to use decimal values, those are included in the table below.

ASCII Table

Decimal	Char	Decimal	Char	Decimal	Char
0	Null	43	+	86	V
1	Start of Heading	44	,	87	W
2	Start of Text	45	-	88	Z
3	End of Text	46	.	89	Y

Decimal	Char	Decimal	Char	Decimal	Char
4	End of Transmission	47	/	90	Z
5	Enquiry	48	0	91	[
6	Acknowledge	49	1	92	\
7	Bell	50	2	93	]
8	Backspace	51	3	94	^
9	Horizontal Tab	52	4	95	_
10	Line Feed	53	5	96	`
11	Vertical Tab	54	6	97	a
12	Form Feed	55	7	98	b
13	Carriage Return	56	8	99	c
14	Shift Out	57	9	100	d
15	Shift In	58	:	101	e
16	Data Link Escape	59	;	102	f
17	Device Control 1	60	<	103	g
18	Device Control 2	61	=	104	h
19	Device Control 3	62	>	105	i
20	Device Control 4	63	?	106	j
21	Negative Acknowledge	64	@	107	k
22	Synchronous Idle	65	A	108	l
23	End of sp. Block	66	B	109	m
24	Cancel	67	C	110	n
25	End of Medium	68	D	111	o
26	Substitute	69	E	112	p
27	Escape	70	F	113	q
28	File Separator	71	G	114	r

Decimal	Char	Decimal	Char	Decimal	Char
29	Group Separator	72	H	115	s
30	Record Separator	73	I	116	t
31	Unit Separator	74	J	117	u
32	Space	75	K	118	v
33	!	76	L	119	w
34	"	77	M	120	x
35	#	78	N	121	y
36	$	79	O	122	z
37	%	80	P	123	{
38	&	81	Q	124		
39	'	82	R	125	}
40	(	83	S	126	~
41	)	84	T	127	Del
42	*	85	U		

As you can see from the table, all of the capital letters are together in order, and the lowercase letters are together. The capital letter *A* is 65 and the lowercase *a* is 97. When the comparisons are made:

> `"Apple" < "apple"` is True because comparing *A* to *a*, 65 < 97 is true.

> `"Apple" == "apple"` is False because 65 does not equal 97.

> `"Apple" > "apple"` is False because 65 is not greater than 97.

If the first character is the same in both strings, the comparison will move to the second character in each string. In the example below, the characters are the same until the *a* in *Grapes* and the *e* in *Great*.

```
book1 = "The Grapes of Wrath"
book2 = "The Great Gatsby"
```

You can set up conditions to determine which string should be processed first using comparisons.

String Built-in Functions

Most programming languages provide **built-in functions** for manipulating strings. As with all of our other functions, built-in and customized, each one also has parentheses.

The structure to use them is: `variableName.function()`

Always check the official documentation for available functions, what they do, and the format needed to use them. There are many more in addition to the ones listed below. Examples will use the variable *message* with the assigned string value below.

```
message = "Programming is fun!"
```

Several frequently used functions are:

`find()`	Searches a string for one or more characters in it.
	Returns the index position where the string starts.
	Returns −1 if the string is not found.
`print(message.find("g"))`	will display 3, which is the index position for *g*.
`print(message.find("z"))`	will display −1 since *z* is not found in the string.
`upper()`	Converts a string to uppercase.

`print(message.upper())`	will display PROGRAMMING IS FUN!
`lower()`	Converts a string to lowercase.
`print(message.lower())`	will display programming is fun!

Both `upper()` and `lower()` are useful when accepting input from the keyboard. You can convert the user input to either upper- or lowercase for use in the program. Then you will not have to check for multiple options depending on what is keyed in. For example, if the user needs to type "yes" to continue, they could type "yes", "Yes", or "YES", among other combinations. If you convert what they type to upper- or lowercase, you only have to compare it to one possibility, either "YES" after using `upper()` or "yes" after using `lower()`.

`If (userVal.lower() == "yes"):`	Accommodates all typing possibilities.
`replace()`	Finds and converts one or more characters with another character or string.
`print(message.replace(" fun", "great"))`	will display Programming is great!
`startswith()`	If the string is found, then the Boolean value *true* is returned. Otherwise, *false* is returned.
`print(message.startswith("P"))`	will display: True
`print(message.startswith("p"))`	will display: False

Remember that strings are immutable (not changeable), so printing these changes does not modify the original variable `message` contents. A copy of the string is returned where applicable, such as with upper() or lower().

REVIEW QUESTIONS

What would be printed in the following lines of code? Type it into Python if you are not sure.

1. artist = "One hit wonder"
   ```
   print(artist[5])
   ```

2. ```
   print(artist[72 - 68])
   ```

3. ```
   print(artist[-3])
   ```

4. ```
   print(artist[len(artist) - 1])
   ```

5. Write some index position examples of your own. Type them into Python to confirm your result.

What is printed in each of the following lines of code?

6. ```
   song = "do re mi "
   print(song + song)
   ```

7. ```
   song = "do re mi "
   print(song * 3)
   ```

8. Create a new variable, *fullName*, by concatenating the variables below:
   ```
   firstName = "Leon"
   middleName = "Ardo "
   lastName = "Da Vinci"
   ```

9. What does the word *immutable* mean?

10. What happens when you try to change a string?

Let's set up a variable named *fact* to be equal to the following string:
```
fact = "Coding is awesome!"
```
```

It's easiest to practice slicing by building a table as we did above with the index position for each character.

value	C	o	d	i	n	g		i	s		a	w	e	s	o	m	e	!
index	0	1	2	3	4	5	6	7	8	9	10	11	12	13	14	15	16	17

What would each of the following produce?

11. `fact[0:8]`

12. `fact[:13]`

13. `fact[13:17]`

14. `fact[15:]`

15. `fact[len(fact) - 8:22]`

16. What is returned by:
```
alert = "Fire alarm test"
alert.find("a")
```

17. What is returned by:
```
alert = "Fire alarm test"
alert.lower()
```

18. How would you change "Fire alarm test" to be "Fire alarm drill"?

19. How would you determine if the user input begins with a *y* in the following code?
```
print("Do you want to continue")
continue = input("Enter 'yes' or 'no':)
```

Flashcard App

12 Input

MUST KNOW

⚡ The `input()` built-in function is used to capture user input from the keyboard.

⚡ The program will pause and wait until the *Enter* key is detected to continue.

⚡ All data coming in from the keyboard is a string data type.

⚡ The `open()` function provides a connection between a program and a data file.

⚡ The *try* and *except* commands are used to protect our program from possible errors.

any times, we want our software program to use data provided by a file or to interact with the user or player if we have a game. That interaction can often be in the form of data being entered. It could be for a guess or a selection from several options.

User Input

Python provides the **input( )** built-in function to capture user input. When Python sees this command, it will pause the program and wait for something to be typed on the keyboard. As soon as it detects that the *Enter* key has been pressed, it will capture the keystrokes up to that point.

We need to store the user input in a variable to use in our program. Otherwise, whatever was typed is not saved and is lost in cyberspace. It is therefore not available to make decisions, select options, display messages, or for other features of your program.

The **input()** command is a built-in function, meaning it comes precoded with Python. You must use the parentheses with built-in functions. With the **input()** function, you have the option to include a message to users about what type of data they should key in. Without a message, the computer simply pauses, and anyone using your program may think it froze when it is actually simply waiting for a response. Also, give clear instructions so the user will have a better chance of entering valid data to start a good user experience.

```
variable = input("Give info about what to type")
name = input("Please enter your first name: ")
choice = input("Please select option a, b, or c ")
```

You can also use the **print()** function to display a message to the user instead of typing the message in the **input()** function.

```
print("Please enter your first name: ")
name = input()
```

The data type of any value typed in from the keyboard is string. Even if you ask the user to type in a number, Python will consider it to be a string. You must convert it to an **int()** or **float()** to use it in mathematical operations. See Chapter 9 for a refresher on casting if needed.

Validate User Input

We should always check to ensure valid data was entered from the keyboard. Python has commands that can be used to check data to ensure it won't cause your program to crash (meaning end abruptly with an error!).

There are two commands that work together: *try* and *except*. You cannot have one without the other. Both of these have a colon (:) after the command. The *try* command attempts to execute a line of code. If there is an error, rather than crashing your program with the error, it will instead execute the code in the *except* block. This gives us, as the programmer, a chance to cushion the error and handle it without crashing.

This makes these very useful for checking user input. No matter who uses your program, if you are allowing input from the keyboard, eventually someone will type invalid data. This gives us a chance to check for an invalid response and respond accordingly. The code in the *except* section will only execute if the code in the *try* section results in an error.

Indentation is how Python knows what lines of code are associated with certain commands. *try* and *except* are two of these commands. The programmer must indent anything that is part of the *try* section under it and the same for the *except*. Notice that *try* and *except* are at the same level of indentation. The code under each is indented one level. When you press the *Enter* key after the colon, Python automatically indents the code one level for you. Make sure the indentation for each line is the same, or you will have a syntax error with this message:

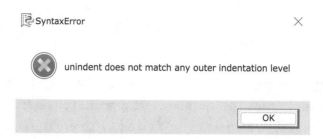

To indicate that the code belonging to the *try* or *except* is finished, you simply unindent the next line of code back one level.

The code in the *try* section will always run, until an error in one of the lines of code occurs. Control immediately passes to the *except* block and anything else in the *try* block is skipped. It is good programming practice to limit the lines of code in the *try* section to just those that need to be checked for potential errors before the program continues. In the example below, we are asking the user to enter numbers. However, it is possible that someone could type "ten" or a symbol by accident. Remember that all data from the keyboard has a string datatype.

> **BTW**
>
> When indenting, do not mix using the tab key and spaces from the space bar. Python will give an error message if this happens:
> `SyntaxError: inconsistent use of tabs and spaces in indentation`

```python
age = input("How old are you? ")
try:
    age = int(age)



    
except:
    print("Invalid data")
```

This checks for valid numbers by casting to an integer. Remember only characters that look like numbers can be successfully cast to an `int` or `float`.

Rather than crashing, the program prints an error message.

We should keep in mind:

- If the user types in 10, then the *try* function works correctly. The *except* code is not run.

- If the user types in the word, ten, then the attempt to convert it to a number fails and the error message in the *except* block is printed. Our program continues normally rather than ending with an error.

Since we have cushioned our program from crashing with invalid data, the program will continue after the *try:/except:* block finishes. Therefore, we need to set a *flag* variable that indicates all is well and we should continue with the program.

```
flag = 0              # Assumes valid data.
level = input("Type 1 for easy, 2 for hard ")
try:
      level = int(level)
except:
      flag = 1        # Triggers the flag variable that invalid data
                      # was received.

                      # continue with the program only if valid data
                      # was received.
if (flag == 1):
      print ("Invalid data entered ")
else:
                      # continue with the program.
```

Reading and Writing Files

Data is everywhere! Data is collected every time we watch a video, click to view an item, purchase an item, return an item, and so much more. Many organizations want to use data collected to better plan and produce items. This data is available in files, so we need to learn how to read the data into our program. You may have heard of **machine learning** and **data analytics**. These are the result of programs reading, filtering, and analyzing data looking for patterns and new information in the data that can be of benefit to whatever organization is involved.

Python requires a connection to be established with a file before it can be used in a program. We use the `open()` built-in function to link the file to our program. The `open()` command needs the name of the file and the mode to open the file passed to it in the parentheses. The modes are:

- Read   *r*   Read only

- Write   *w*   Write only, overwriting any existing data

- Append   *a*   Write data to the end of a file, without overwriting data already in the file

- Read and Write   *r+*   Allow read and write access to a file

Read is the default mode. This means if you do not specify a mode, read will be used.

`open()` sends a value to the program that must be stored in a variable. It is used to manage our actions with the file and is referred to as the **Handle**. The *with* keyword ensures the file is closed when processing is finished.

```
with open("speech.txt", "r")as fileIn:
```
fileIn is the file handle.

```
line = fileIn.read()
```
Use the file handle with file functions.

```
print(line)
```

There are three different read commands. The first, `read()`, will read in the entire file. This is risky with large files as it could use up all of your computer's available resources. Your computer would then freeze, and you'll need to restart it.

There is an option to include a parameter for the size in the parentheses.

`print (fileIn.read())`   This version prints the entire file using **read()**.

`print(fileIn.read(50))`   This reads in 50 characters of the file and prints them.

The second type of read command is **readline()**. Only one line from the file will be read in at a time. If our file is four lines, **readline()** would have to be used four times to read in each line. A loop is a great way to read in each line. In Chapter 18 we'll see more on loops.

`print(fileIn.readline())`

The last method, **readlines()** (notice the *s* at the end of the command), will read the file and store each line as an element in a list. We'll talk more about lists in Chapter 16.

`speechList = fileIn.readlines()`

Python will assume your input file is in the same folder as your program unless you provide the path for it to follow as part of the filename. You will see the following error message if the file is not in the folder or the path is incorrect.

```
with open("c:\PyPrograms\testFile.txt", "r")
   as fileIn:
FileNotFoundError: [Errno 2] No such file or
   directory: 'testFile.txt'
```

When you write to a file, you can only write text fields or strings. If you have numbers to write, you can cast them to the *string* data type. When you write to a file, whatever is currently in the file will be overwritten unless you use read/write access r+.

`num = 42`

`num = str(num)`   Casts the integer data type to be a string.

`with open("speech.txt", "w") as fileOut:`

`    fileOut.write(num)`   Writes the string.

Similar to `readlines()`, there is also a `writelines()`, which will write each element of a list to a file. If you open a file to write to it, the file will be created if it does not already exist.

Most programs will need input either through reading a file or from a user providing input. We have commands to read in the data in both cases. An important feature of any program should be to ensure data is valid before continuing to process it, regardless of how it makes its way into a program.

BTW

There is **not** an equivalent to `readline()` when writing to a file.

REVIEW QUESTIONS

1. Why should you store a value the user/player types in a variable?

2. What does the `input()` command do?

3. Write an input command asking the user to guess a number between 1 and 10.

4. What is the purpose of the *try:/except:* structure?

5. How is indentation used with Python?

6. When will the code under the *except* command run?

7. Can you have an *except* statement without a *try*?

8. What punctuation is used with the *try* and *except* statements?

9. What does a flag variable do?

10. Write the code to:
    Ask a user for input about the current temperature.
    Use the try:/except: structure to check for valid input.
    Use an appropriate error message if their input was invalid.

11. Where should you put a flag variable in your answer to question 10?

12. What, if anything, is wrong with the code below?

```
age = input("Please enter your age: ")
try:
age = int(age)
except:
print("Error: Age must be a whole number.")
flag = 1
```

13. What does the **open()** command do?

14. What does the write mode do?

15. What is the difference in write and append?

16. Write the line of code to open a file for reading.

Flashcard App

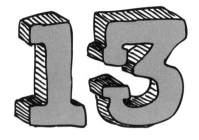

Three Types of Statements

MUST ⚡ KNOW

⚡ Programs are written with a combination of three types of programming statements.

⚡ Sequential statements run and, when finished, execute the next line of code, one after the other.

⚡ Selection statements start with the keyword *if* and only run certain lines of code when a condition is true.

⚡ Repetitive statements repeat a specified number of times or as long as a condition is met.

I have been holding on to this surprise. You can write any program with a combination of only three types of statements! Combining them can be as simple or as complex as your program needs, but it still only takes three different types!

Sequential Statements

The first type of statement is **Sequential**. Just as the word means, the program commands execute one by one. When the command ahead of it completes, the next command begins. The lines of code must also be in the correct sequence to run correct program code. For example, if we had an algorithm to run a production line, the steps must be in the correct order or chaos could occur!

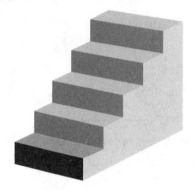

Selection Statements

The second type of statement is a **Selection** statement. These are also referred to as "conditional" statements. Remember how our flowchart had a *decision* shape (the diamond)? It always had two possible outcomes: yes or no. These represent our selection statements, which filter out certain code based on a "condition" set up to evaluate. If the condition is true (yes outcome of the decision), then a block of code is run. If the condition is false (no outcome of the decision), the code is skipped. These commands always start with the keyword *if*. We will look at this in more detail in the next chapter.

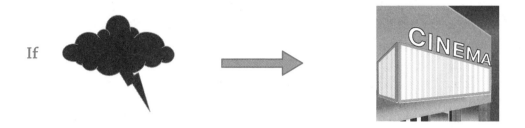

Repetitive Statements

The third type of statement is called a **Repetitive** statement. These are also called iterative statements or loops. These statements will repeat a block of code as long as the programmer specifies. There are several types of iterative statements, and we will look at the most common in future chapters.

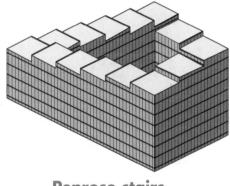

Penrose stairs

REVIEW QUESTIONS

1. Which type of statement starts with the keyword *if*?

2. Which type of statement runs the same block of code over and over?

3. What is the third type of statement that runs the next line of code once it finishes?

Flashcard App

14 Selection Statements

MUST KNOW

⚡ Selection statements, which start with the keyword *if*, involve a true or false condition. The true or false value is the *Boolean value*.

⚡ Code associated with the *if* statement will only run when the condition is true.

⚡ The *else* statement can be used to execute code when the condition for the selection statement is false.

⚡ The *elif* statement is used in Python to provide a way to test multiple possibilities for a condition.

⚡ Programming languages check each condition in order until one of them is true. The code associated with that condition is executed and any remaining possibilities are skipped.

As mentioned in the last chapter, selection statements start with the keyword *if.* This is the way we speak when we use these naturally. If it is a school holiday, then turn off your alarm clock, or at least set it for later!.

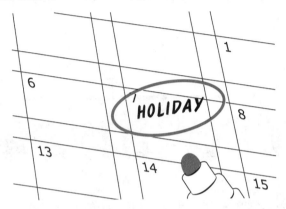

Associated with the *if* is a condition. The condition is evaluated to see if it is true or false. If it is true, then any code associated with the *if* statement is executed. If it is false, then that code is skipped and the program continues with the line of code after all the code associated with the *if* statement.

if the temperature is greater than 80 degrees Fahrenheit
    wear a short-sleeved shirt

This is how the selection statements filter out certain lines of code based on a situation:

> if there are grapes
>> eat grapes

You cannot eat grapes if you do not have any!

Boolean Values

Boolean values are conceptually very simple. They are either true or false. Therefore, Boolean values work well with selection statements. The condition will always evaluate to one of our Boolean values, either true or false.

Remember from our earlier chapter, with binary we only have two values to use: 0 and 1. Since computers use binary to run our code, Boolean values work well with this structure.

> True = 1
>
> False = 0

Several examples of true/false conditions

> Day is Wednesday
>
> Is leap year
>
> Weather is stormy
>
> I can legally drive

Relational Operators

To finish setting up our selection statement, we need to use **relational operators**. That's just a fancy name for terms we use in math and spoken language daily.

> greater than

< less than

>= greater than or equal to

<= less than or equal to

Notice these look a little different than they do in math. We do not have the keys with the math version on our standard keyboards.

Be sure you type these in the order that you say them, meaning "greater than or equal to" places the greater than sign first, then the equals sign. The symbols will not be recognized if you type them in the opposite order, and the interpreter will display an error message.

== equal to. Python uses two equal signs for comparison.

Several popular programming languages use two equal signs for a comparison with conditionals. This distinguishes it from the single equal sign, which is used to assign a value to a variable.

!= not equal to

Many programming languages, including Python, use the exclamation mark for the "not" sign.

Format of the Selection Statement Condition

Now we have all the pieces needed to build our condition. Let's say we want to build a condition to determine when to feed the dog. I feed my dogs at

6:00 p.m. One of them will start nudging me for dinner starting at 5:30, if not earlier! My condition is, if it is 6:00 p.m., then feed the dogs.

To write that in Python code, we start with the *if* keyword.

```
if
```

Then we add the condition. We use the double equals sign notation since we are doing a comparison to see if it is 6:00 p.m. Notice the use of parentheses around the condition. Python does not require the parentheses, but it is not an issue if they are there. Many other frequently used programming languages require parentheses around conditions, so it is a good habit to go ahead and start using them. It will make the transition to a new programming language potentially easier.

```
if (time == 1800)
```
Notice the use of military time to distinguish a.m. from p.m.

Python has punctuation after the condition to signal the end of the condition. Python uses the : or colon. If you press the *Enter* key after typing in the colon, Python will automatically indent the next line.

```
if (time == 1800):
```
The colon is at the end of the condition.

Python is very particular about indentation. Any code that should be executed when the condition is true must be indented under the *if* statement. While other languages do not require the indentation, good programming practice dictates indenting code under the corresponding *if* statement for readability. Other languages also often require braces, {}, wrapped around the code to execute when the *if* condition is true. Python uses indentation instead. To indicate the end of code that should run when the condition is true, the first line of code not associated with the *if* condition is moved back a level to be even with the indentation level of the *if* keyword.

All lines of code that should be executed when the condition is true must be indented underneath the *if* statement.

```
if (time == 1800):
  print("Feed the dogs!")
```

If it is the first of the month, I also give them their heartworm preventive medication.

```
if (day == 1):
  print("Give heartworm pill!")
```

Notice if it is not 6:00 p.m., I do not see the message to feed the dogs. Similarly, if it is not the first of the month, I do not see the reminder to give them their heartworm pills because those lines of code will not execute.

Here is another example with multiple lines of code to execute when the condition is true. Each line is indented one level under the *if* statement.

```
if (day == "Monday"):
  setAlarm = 700
```
Line will execute when the condition is true – indented.

```
  setCoffeePotOn = 715
```
Line will execute when the condition is true – indented.

```
  print("Alarm is set")
```
This line is not part of the selection statement and is not indented under the *if* statement. It will always run.

As we saw in the BTW sidebar in Chapter 12, don't mix spaces and use of the tab key when indenting code. You will get the following error if you do:

```
SyntaxError: inconsistent use of tabs and spaces
   in indentation
```

What Happens When the Condition Is False?

The *if* selection statement is powerful all on its own. However, what happens if we want to do one thing when the condition is true and something else when it is false? So far, we have not done anything when the condition was false. Fortunately, we have a command for this. It's called the *else* statement. Just as the code associated with the *if* statement only executes when the condition is true, the code linked to the *else* statement only executes when the condition is false.

The *else* statement does not have a condition to test. Since we are working with Boolean values, true and false, we know the code associated with the *else* executes only when the condition is false.

With *if/else* blocks, when the condition being tested is true, the program will not even look at the *else* block. The *else* will only be run when the condition is false. Otherwise, it is skipped. The *else* statement also has a colon after it, just like the *if* statement. Notice that the *else* statement lines up indentation-wise with the *if*. Any code to be executed as part of the *else* must be indented one level. The *else* is finished when the next line of code is unindented one level, or the program ends.

```
if ( age >= 21):
  print("You are eligible to vote.")
else:
  print("You must be 21 and registered to vote.")
```

In this example, only one of the messages will print since the conditions are mutually exclusive.

- When **age** is 18, then the condition is false, and the message under the *else* will be printed.

- When **age** is 30, the condition evaluates to true, and the message under the *if* will be printed.

What happens if age equals 21? The condition will still be true since it is set up as age greater than *or* equal to 21. Therefore, the message under the *if* will print in this case. This is an example of testing a boundary condition that we talked about in the chapter on testing.

```
if (thunderstorm):
        print ("Go to the movies.")
else:
        print("Go swimming.")
```

You cannot have an *else* statement without an *if* statement. A syntax error occurs when this happens.

As shown when we introduced the selection statement, you *can* have an *if* statement without an *else*.

Multiple Possibilities: Nesting

There are often cases where there are multiple possibilities in a condition. Think about converting a number grade to a letter grade. Depending on the student's number average, the letter grade could be an *A*, *B*, *C*, *D*, or an *F*. Can an *if* condition handle all those possibilities? Why, yes, it can!

We now introduce the else if statement. Python uses a shortcut version of else if: *elif*. It is used in conjunction with an *if* when there are multiple options. Using our letter grade example, let's set up the conditions.

```
if (average >= 90):
        print ("Grade: A")
elif (average >= 80):
        print ("Grade: B")
elif (average >= 75):
        print ("Grade: C")
elif (average >= 70):
        print("Grade: D")
```

```
else:
    print("Grade: F")
```

There is no limit on the number of *elif* statements you can have in a Python program.

Notice that each *elif* has a condition to evaluate. Only the *else* statement does not have a condition. As with the *if* and *else* statements, the *elif* has punctuation, a colon, after the condition. Also, like the *if* and *else*, any code associated with an *elif* is indented one level underneath it. If you press *Enter* after the colon, Python will indent the next line by the correct amount.

Once a condition evaluates to be true, the code associated with that condition is run and the rest of the *elif* conditions are not tested. The selection statement is over at that point. The program continues with the next line of code after the complete *if* statement or terminates the program if there are no other lines of code. Using our Grade condition, if our average is 78, then the condition associated with the *if* is tested. It is false, so the program continues and tests the condition with the first *elif* statement. It is false, so the condition with the second *elif* statement is tested. It is true, so Grade: C is printed, and the selection statement is over. The remaining *elif* condition is not tested. The *else* is also skipped.

Note that you could write multiple *if* statements rather than use an *if/elif* structure. However, each individual *if* statement's condition would be evaluated. Every condition that is true would then run the code associated with it. This is less efficient, especially if you have large data sets to process. It could also produce unexpected results. For example, let's rewrite our letter grade code to use multiple *if* statements and see what happens.

```
if (average >= 90):
    print ("Grade: A")
if (average >= 80):
    print ("Grade: B")
if (average >= 75):
```

```
      print ("Grade: C")
if (average >= 70):
      print("Grade: D")
if (average < 70):
```
We would need to add a condition that used to be with the *else*.
```
      print("Grade: F")
```

In this case, if our average was 92, then each letter grade would print because each condition would be true.

Selection statements are very powerful and provide the ability to test many conditions, allowing us to provide many features and flexibility in a program. Using an *if/elif/else* structure makes our code readable and efficient too.

REVIEW QUESTIONS

1. Are the following Boolean conditions?
   a. A coin flip lands on heads.
   b. Are the lights on?
   c. Is it time to clean your room?
   d. What day is it?

2. Write a selection statement that tests if you have a sibling. When the condition is true, print a message stating you have siblings.

3. Write a selection statement that tests if you can whistle. If it is true, print a message that you can whistle.

4. What is the sign for greater than?

5. What is the symbol for less than or equal to?

6. Why are two equal signs used?

7. Write the selection statement to test if a song is your favorite.

8. What punctuation goes at the end of an *if* statement in Python?

9. Are the parentheses around an *if* statement required by Python?

10. How do we tell Python what to do if the condition is true?

11. Write a selection statement to set your alarm only for school days.

12. Write a selection statement to wash the dogs if they swam in the lake.

13. Describe what this condition is testing.

```
if (price >= $100):
    print ("Not today")
else:
    print ("Sold! ")
```

14. Describe what this condition is testing.

```
if (onTime):
    print("Caught the school bus!")
else:
    print("Late for school.")
```

15. Write a condition to determine whether to listen to a song that is playing or to skip it.

16. Write a condition to buy new shoes for school if yours are wearing out.

17. If a condition is false, will the block of code associated with it execute?

18. How is Python notified that a selection statement is done?

19. What is the following pseudocode doing?

```
if (time is 6:00 p.m.)
    feed the dog
play with the dog
brush dog
```

20. Does each condition in an *if/elif* statement get evaluated?

21. What happens when more than one condition is true with an *if/elif* statement?

22. What will the result of this code be?
```
game = "tennis"
if (game == "volleyball"):
   print ("Best 3 of 5 games")
elif (game == "basketball"):
   print ("Two halves")
elif (game == "hockey"):
   print ("Three periods")
elif (game == "baseball"):
   print("Nine Innings")
else:
   print("Check the rule book")
```

23. Write the code to add 10 to a number if the modulus value is 0 and add 5 to it if the modulus value is 1 when a number is divisible by 3.

Use the following variables for the next question.
```
book1 = "Jane Eyre"
book2 = "Jane Seymour"
book3 = "Jane"
```

24. What does this block of code print?
```
if (book1 < book2):
   print ("Shelve", book1, "first")
else:
   print ("Shelve", book2, "first")
```

25. What, if anything, is wrong with this code?
```
avg = 87
threshold = 90
if (avg => threshold)
   print("You qualify!")
else
   print("Try again.")
```

Flashcard App

15 Logical Operators

ometimes, we need more than one event to be true for our condition to be true. There is a way to do this in programming as well! We use logical operators for this. There are three that we use.

Logical Operator: *and*

Some programming languages, such as Java, use two ampersands, &&, to represent *and*. Python uses the word *and* in lowercase.

When you combine two conditions with an *and*, both conditions must evaluate to true for the total condition to be true. A common mistake students make at first is thinking both conditions have to be the same and assume the entire condition is true when both sides are false as well. This is incorrect! It's only when both conditions are true. It's like a Venn diagram with the overlapping area of two circles representing *and*.

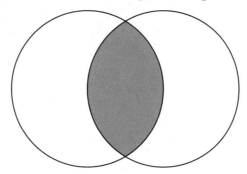

For example, assume we have two variables: *fahrenheit* and *storm*.

```
if (fahrenheit >= 80 and storm == False):
    print ("Let's go to the pool!")
```

Both conditions must be true for us to go to the pool.

In this example, notice that we don't have to test for *registeredToVote ==* *True*. We can just write *regeredToVote*. It's like stating: *if True* for that condition.

```
if (age >= 21 and registeredToVote):
    print ("Be sure to vote in the election.")
```

Logical Operator: *or*

Sometimes, we only need one of several events to be true for our condition to be true. Our second logical operator is *or*. Some programming languages, such as Java, use two vertical lines, ||, to represent *or*. (This is a single perpendicular line key typed twice and is usually found above the *Enter* key.) Python uses the keyword *or*.

When you combine two conditions with an *or*, only one of the conditions must be true for the entire condition to be true. It's like a Venn diagram with the total area of two circles representing *or*.

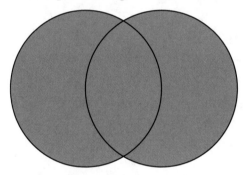

In this example, if it is either 6:00 a.m. **or** 6:00 p.m., then it is time to feed my dogs.

```
if (time == 0600 or time == 1800):
    print ("Feed the dogs!")
```

Here's another example.

```
if (day == "Saturday" or day == "Sunday" ):
    print ("It is the weekend! ")
```

Note that both conditions can be true with an *or* compound condition. The only time an *or* condition is false is when both conditions evaluate to false.

Logical Operator: *not*

Sometimes, we need the opposite of an event for our condition. There is a way to do this as well! This logical operator is *not*. The exclamation point, !, can also be used in Python to represent *not*.

When you use *not*, if the condition was true, *not* makes it false and vice versa. For example, if the variable storm is true, then *not* makes the condition false, and we will go to the swimming pool.

```
if (not storm):
        print ("Go to the pool!")
```

In this condition, when the variable song equals the string "favorite", *not* makes the condition false, and the song will not be played because it is not a favorite one.

```
if (not (song == "favorite")):
            print ("Skip song.")
```

Another way to write this is:

```
if (song != "favorite"):
```

My students generally find this version easier to understand, but both are correct.

Combining Logical Operators

We can combine logical operators to make more complex conditions. Be sure to use parentheses to be clear about what belongs together. Evaluate each condition separately, then combine the conditions inside parentheses with their associated logical operator. Keep building the outcome of the conditions and logical operators to determine the ultimate Boolean value, true or false.

```
if (not(month == "June" and month == "July"
and month == "August")):
    print ("School is in session.")
```

With the above condition, if month is "May", then the condition is true and the phrase will be printed.

If month is "July", then the condition is false and nothing will be printed.

Here's another example. See if you can understand what this condition tests before reading about it.

```
if ((country == "USA" or country == "UK" or
country == "Canada") and (speedLimit <= 70)):
    print ("Speed limit is in miles per hour.")
```

In this example, if the variable country has the value "UK" and the speedLimit is less than or equal to 70, then the "miles per hour" message will be printed.

If country is "Canada" and the speedLimit is 82, then nothing will be printed.

The use of conditions makes the selection statement one of the most used and powerful statements. The use of the relational and logical operators allows us to create complex conditions to test anything our program needs.

REVIEW QUESTIONS

1. When are *or* conditions true?

2. When are *and* conditions false?

3. When will the following condition be true?
```
if (time == 1700 and !rain):
    print ("Walk the dogs!")
```

4. When will the following condition be true?
```
if (day == "Saturday" and time == 1300):
    print("Time to watch my favorite series!")
```

Use the following variables for the next question.
```
book1 = "Jane Eyre"
book2 = "Jane Seymour"
book3 = "Jane"
```

5. What does this code print?
```
if (book2 <= book1) and (book3 < book2):
    nextToShelve = book3
    print("Shelve", nextToShelve, "next")
```

6. Write a condition to test if someone is a fan of classic rock and plays the guitar.

7. Write a condition to test if it is time to clean the fish tank based on a weekend day and the number of elapsed days since the last cleaning is more than ten.

8. What is printed in the following code if today is Wednesday at 7:00 p.m.?
```
if (time == 0700 or day == "Monday")
    print ("Coffee is ready!")
else:
    print("The coffeepot is not turned on.")
```

9. Write a compound selection statement to decide whether to watch TV based on the time of day.

10. Write a statement to narrow your college search based on whether a school's ranking is between 1 and 50 and it is a state-supported (public) school.

11. Describe what the following code is doing:

```
if (not(lives == 0)):
    print ("Play on!")
else:
    print("Play again?")
```

12. Write a selection statement to test if a movie you want to see is playing and if you do not have the money for a ticket, ask for extra chores to earn the money.

13. Write a selection statement to level up when the player has solved all the challenges using *not*.

14. Write the code to print that a new high score has been reached if the player wins and the score is greater than the current high score.

Flashcard App

16 Lists

hat is a list? Think about a grocery list or to-do list. You write items down either physically or digitally so you will have them all available to you when needed, such as when you are at the grocery store.

All of the items in that list are associated with one name, such as a grocery list. This works the same way in programming. The variables we have used so far can only hold one value at a time. Rather than have many variables to hold each item separately, we can just use one variable name and define it as a list.

In Python, the programmer decides on a name for the list and defines it in this format:

```
list_Name = list ()
```

In Python, we can also define a list and load values into it at the same time. We use square brackets around its values. Individual values in the list are separated by a comma.

```
                                              # List of string values
grocery = ["bread", "milk", "grapes"]
                                              # List of integers
testGrades = [100, 96, 88, 92, 84, 80]
                                              # List of floats
temperature = [92.0, 76.2, 87.5, 90.5, 91.7]
                                              # Creates an empty list
roster = []
```

Many programming languages only accept one datatype in each list, similar to the ones above. Python, however, allows different datatypes in the same list. The one named *color* has two strings, an integer, and even a list of numbers. Note that the list element, [255, 0, 0], only count as one element in the *color* list.

```
color = ["red", "#ff0000", [255, 0, 0]]
```

Here is another example of a partial list of presidents' last names.

```
roster = ["Washington", "Adams", "Jefferson"]
```

How to Reference an Item in a List

Sometimes, we want to use the full list, and sometimes, we want to use an individual item in a list. The members of the list are called **Elements**. Each element has a position in the list. The position is an integer and is called an **Index Value**.

Here is a list of numbers in a list named *lockers*. The data values in the list are in the top row. The index position of each value is in the bottom row. Notice the first index position is 0!

value	101	202	303	404	505	606	707	808	909	1010
index	0	1	2	3	4	5	6	7	8	9

If we want to refer to an element using Python, we type the list name and use square brackets, [ ], around the index position.

```
List_Name[index_Position]
```

From the list of numbers above, the last item in the list is the value 1010 at index position 9. We access this element as:

```
lockers[9]
```

Using our earlier list of a class roster:

```
roster = ["Washington", "Adams", "Jefferson"]
```

BTW

Here is an odd thing about programming languages. Most of them, Python included, start counting lists at index position 0. There are a few new languages that start at 1, so that will be something to review when you learn a new programming language.

We can refer to the first element in the list like this:

```
roster[0]
```

We may want to print the element:

```
print(roster[0])
```

will display

```
Washington
```

If we want to change an element, we use this format:

```
roster[1] = "John Adams"
```

This will change the value at index position 1 to overwrite "Adams" with "John Adams".

You cannot change the index position in a list. These are assigned by Python as new elements are added or others are removed. You *can* change the value of an element at a specified index.

Lists: Length

We often need to know how long a list is. The size of it can vary based on whether elements are being added to the list or removed from it. Fortunately, there is a built-in function we can use to learn the length of a list without having to manually count the number of elements. While we could count how many elements are in smaller lists, such as my class roster, datasets can get very large and humans simply cannot effectively and efficiently process large datasets. Computers were made for activities like this!

The function is `len()` which is short for length. This is the same `len()` function we saw in Chapter 11 when we wanted to find out how many characters were in a string. The name of the list is provided in the parentheses as an argument. `len()` returns an integer with the length or size of the list. In the example below, the value returned is stored in the variable *howBig*.

```
howBig = len(roster)
```

This part gets a little confusing. Even though the list starts at 0 with its index position, the `len()` command is the number of elements. We start counting at 1, and the length is how many total elements are in the list.

In our earlier example, our length is 3 because we have 3 elements in our list.

```
roster = ["Washington", "Adams", "Jefferson"]
```

The index positions are 0, 1, and 2.

value	Washington	Adams	Jefferson
index	0	1	2

With the `len()` function, we are able to refer to the index position of the last item in a list as:

```
list_Name[len(list_Name) - 1]
```

With our list, *roster,* we can refer to the last item in either format:

```
roster[2]
roster[len(roster) - 1]
```

This is often a difficult concept for new programmers to grasp, so do not worry if you need to think about it a while.

Concatenation

Lists work the same way as strings with concatenation. If I have two lists, I can glue them together using the + symbol.

```
list1 = [1, 3, 5]
list2 = ["a ", "b ", "c "]
list3 = list1 + list2
print(list3)
```

      # This is the output from concatenating list1 and list2.

```
[1, 3, 5, 'a ', 'b ', 'c ']
```

Python is smart enough to know that the plus sign means addition when the datatypes are numbers, either integers or floats (numbers with decimals), and to use concatenation when the datatypes are strings or lists.

You will get an error if you try to use the + symbol as addition with lists. If we try the following line of code:

```
list4 = list1 + 1
```

We get the following error that tells us we cannot concatenate an integer to a list, so Python thinks we are using concatenation versus addition. The error message also politely reminds us that we can only concatenate a list to another list. Thanks, Python!

```
TypeError: can only concatenate list (not
"int") to list
```

You can also use the multiplication sign, *, with lists just like we can with strings. Again, Python is smart enough to recognize that, with both strings and lists, this operator * means to duplicate them the number of times indicated.

```
print(list2 * 3)          # will produce
['a', 'b', 'c', 'a', 'b', 'c', 'a', 'b', 'c']
```

We can even use the multiplication sign with lists to store the new value, not just print it. This example takes the current value of the variable address, duplicates it, and stores the result back in the same variable, overwriting the previous value.

```
address = address * 5
print(address)
440440440440440
```

```
list5 = list2 * 3
print(list5)
'a', 'b', 'c', 'a', 'b', 'c', 'a', 'b', 'c'
```

Note that subtraction, −, and division, /, do not have equivalent functions with lists.

Slicing

Programs often need to work with a section of a list. Python does this using a technique called slicing, just as we used with strings. The format in Python is:

```
listName[start:stop]
```

Start represents the index position to start the selection or slice. It is *inclusive*, meaning the element at that position in the list is included in the selection.

Stop represents the index position to stop the slice. It is *exclusive*, meaning the character at that position is *not* included.

```
games = ["Mario Cart", "Fortnite",
         "Minecraft", "Tetris", "Rocket
         League", "Pong"]
```

`print(games[0:2])` would print:

      Mario Cart, Fortnite

Mario Cart is at index position 0, and it is included with slicing.
Index position 2 is excluded.
So we start at index 0, include index position 1, but do not include index 2.

`print(games[3:5])` would print:

      Tetris, Rocket League

Index position 3 contains the game "Tetris".

We take the elements up to but *not* including the one at index 5.

If you leave the starting position blank, then the slice starts at the beginning of the list.

`games[:4]` results in:

Mario Cart, Fortnite, Minecraft, Tetris

Our string slice includes the games at indices 0, 1, 2, and 3.

If you leave the ending position blank, then the slice goes all the way to the end of the list.

`games[4:]` results in:

Rocket League, Pong

Leaving both blank would select the entire list: `games[:]`

Just as with strings, even though we get an `IndexError: list index out of range error` when we use an index position that is too large when referencing an element in a list, with slicing, you can reference an index position that does not exist for the list, and you will not receive an error!

With our list of *games* example, if we type:

```
games[8]          # List index out of range error occurs.
g1 = games[8:9]   # Note that the numbers used in our
                  # slice are out of the range of our list.
```

If we print g1, then nothing is displayed on our output console.

```
print(g1)
```

We can get a better picture of what is going on by printing the length of our variable g1. We use the built-in function `len()` to see the length.

```
print(len(g1))
0
```

The length of our list g1 is 0. This is because our slice used values 8:9 that are outside of the size of our list. The variable g1 was created, but it is empty, and we did not get a "list index out of range" error!

Similarly, if we start our slice with a value too large for our list and do not include an ending position, we do not get an error, and the new slice is empty with a length of 0.

```
g2 = games[11:]
print(len(g2))
0
```

Again, if we try to reference an index position without slicing that is not in our list, then we get the IndexError.

This example is not slicing. It is only referencing the element at index position 11.

```
g3 = games[11]
IndexError: list index out of range
```

Processing Lists

We will often need to check every item in a list. We may have a selection statement that will process the elements that meet a certain condition, but we need to check each element to see if it meets the criteria. Fortunately, the *for* loop is a perfect use for this!

The *for* loop will automatically start at the beginning of the list and not stop until each element in the list has been accessed. (We'll talk more about loops in Chapter 18.)

```
roster = ["Washington", "Adams", "Jefferson"]
for name in roster:
    if (name == "Adams"):
        print (name)
```

iteration	name
1	Washington
2	Adams
3	Jefferson

The first time through the loop, the iteration variable, *name*, takes on the value "Washington". The *if* statement then checks to see if *name* equals "Adams". It does not, so Python goes back up to the top of the *for* loop.

The second time through, the iteration variable, *name*, holds the value "Adams". The *if* statement then checks to see if *name* equals "Adams", which it does. Therefore, the *print* statement is executed, and the current value of *name*, which is "Adams", is printed.

We go back to the top of the *for* loop, and now the variable *name* holds the value "Jefferson". The *if* statement then checks to see if *name* equals "Adams". The *name* does not match "Adams", so Python moves back to the top of the *for* statement.

This time, Python recognizes that all items in the list were accessed, so it completes the loop and goes to the next line of code after the *for* loop or ends the program if that was the last line of code.

Lists: Frequently Used Built-in Functions

Since lists are commonly used in Python and other programming languages, many modules of code to work with lists have already been written and included with Python as built-in functions and methods. This chapter presents several that you will probably need when processing lists because they are commonly used. However, always check the online documentation for a list of the built-in functions provided and any parameters they have.

Mutable is a word that means changeable, as in mutate. You may recall that strings are immutable, but Python allows us to change the elements in a list. For example, to change "apple" to be "banana":

```
fruit = ["apple", "grapes"]
fruit[0] = "banana"
print(fruit)
['banana', 'grapes']      # Output of the print statement
```

The keyword **in** will check to see if a data value is included in a list. If the value is *in* the list, then True is returned. Otherwise, False is returned. Using our fruit list above:

```
if ("grapes" in fruit):
    print("grapes are in the fruit list")
```

sort() will change the list to be sorted in ascending order. The format is:

```
listName.sort()
```

EXAMPLE

```
nums = [5, 3, 77, 21, 95, 0, -5, 29]
nums.sort()
print(nums)
[-5, 0, 3, 5, 21, 29, 77, 95]    # The sorted list
```

`append()` is a built-in function that adds an element to the *end* of a list. The format is:

`listName.append(dataToAppend)`

► `roster.append("Madison")`

Keep in mind that you can only append one element at a time.

Another frequently needed function to use with lists is to insert a value at a particular position in a list. `insert()` is a built-in function that adds an element to a specified location in a list. The format is:

`listName.insert(indexLocation, dataToInsert)`

► If our list of presidents is below:

```
roster = ["Washington", "Adams",
"Jefferson", "Madison", "Monroe", "Van
Buren"]
```

We realize we forgot to include President Jackson! We can insert his name in the proper location.

```
roster.insert(5, "Jackson")
```

► Remember, while Jackson was the 6th president, our list starts at index position 0, so his name should be inserted at the 5th index location. Our list is now:

```
roster = ["Washington", "Adams",
"Jefferson", "Madison", "Monroe",
"Jackson", "Van Buren"]
```

▶ Notice that when we inserted "Jackson", Python did not overwrite the existing value at index position 5. Instead, Python took care of moving the existing value, "Van Buren", one position to the right. Note that we can only insert one element at a time with this function.

There are times when we need to remove items from our lists. Python provides several ways to do this. With each of these methods, Python shifts any elements in the list after the one removed down a position. Our list length is now reduced by one as well.

```
remove(element)
pop(index)
del
```

The *remove(element)* function searches for and removes the value specified in the parentheses. If the element is not found in the list, then a "ValueError" message is displayed. Therefore, you should search for an element first to ensure it is in the list or use a *try:/except:* structure as discussed in Chapter 12. Using the list of numbers below:

```
nums = [1, 99, 24, 7, 44, 17, 29, 44]
```

`nums.remove(44)` will remove the first occurrence of the number 44 from the list. Our list is now:

```
nums = [1, 99, 24, 7, 17, 29, 44]
```

`pop()` will return and remove the element at a given index position. If an index value is not provided, then the last item in the list is returned and removed.

```
numbers = [12.5, 42.2, 60.0, 87.4, 33.3]
```

`numbers.pop(3)` removes and returns the value 87.4, which was stored in index position 3. Remember that lists start at index position 0. Our numbers list is now:

```
numbers = [12.5, 42.2, 60.0, 33.3]
```

Another `pop()` example without an index position specified; `numbers.pop()` removes and returns 33.3. Our numbers list is now:

```
numbers = [12.5, 42.2, 60.0]
```

`del listName[index value]` deletes the item at the specified index position. If we use our list of presidents:

```
roster = ["Washington", "Adams", "Jefferson",
"Madison", "Monroe", "Jackson", "Van Buren"]
```

`del roster[4]` will remove "Monroe" and our list will be:

```
roster = ["Washington", "Adams", "Jefferson",
"Madison", "Jackson", "Van Buren"]
```

Other frequently needed functions to use with lists are finding the largest and smallest elements in the list. While we could write our own code to loop through all the values and compare them to see which is the largest or smallest, the code is already written, so let's use it!

`max()` is a built-in function that finds and returns the largest number in a list. The format is:

```
max(listName)
```

If we have a list of random numbers like the one below:

```
nums = [1, 99, 24, 7, 44, -17, 29]
big = max(nums)
```

This will return the value 99 and store it in the variable named *big*. Similarly, `min()` is a built-in function that finds and returns the smallest number in a list. If we have another list of random numbers, this time decimal numbers or floats in Python:

```
numbers = [12.5, -42.2, 60.0, -87.4, 33.3]
small = min(numbers)
```

This will return the number −87.4 and store it in the variable named *small*. *max()* and **min()** also work with lists of strings. The comparison is based on the alphabetic letters.

```
notes = ["do", "re", "mi", "fa", "so", "la",
"ti", "do"]
print(max(notes))
ti
print(min(notes))
do
```

Another frequently needed function to use with lists is summing all of the elements in the list. While we could also write our own loop to do this, the code is already written, so there is no need to reinvent the wheel!

sum() is a built-in function that totals all of the number in a list. The format is:

```
sum(listName)
```

Using the lists below:

```
nums = [1, 99, 24, 7, 44, 17, 29]
numbers = [12.5, 42.2, 60.0, 87.4, 33.3]
total = sum(nums)
```

This will return the value 221 and store it in the variable named *total*.

```
amount = sum(numbers)
```

This will return the value 235.4 and store it in the variable named *amount*.

Note that the **sum()** function only works with numbers. If you try to use it with strings, an error will occur.

split() will separate a string and create a list with each word as an element. It will use a space by default to determine when a new element begins, but you can provide the character to use for the split as an argument.

```
news = "This is where the magic begins!"
newsList = news.split()
print(newsList)        # We have a list of each word.
['This', 'is', 'where', 'the', 'magic',
'begins!']
amenities = "wifi:pool:shuttle"
amenities2 = amenities.split(":")
print(amenities2) # split() creates a list using the colon as
                    the separator character.
['wifi', 'pool', 'shuttle']
```

There are many uses for lists in computer science. Intuitively, they are easy to understand and manipulate with the *for* loop and the built-in functions provided along with any code you need to add.

REVIEW QUESTIONS

1. Define a list named *movies* with three of your favorite movies in it.

2. Define a list named *me* and include four details about you, such as height, age, or eye color.

3. What are individual items in a list called?

4. How do we reference an individual item in a list?

5. What is the first index position in a Python list?

6. Create a list of at least four elements that are your favorite foods.
    Print the list.
    Change one item in the list to a different food.
    Print the list again to see the updates.

7. Given the list below, write the code to find its length.
    Print the list length and the element at the last index position.

    ```
    scores = [141, 96, 21, 53, 99, 103, 78, -84,
        47, 72, 1023, 815, 914, 1029, 55]
    ```

8. Create a list of five of your favorite songs.
    Process the list using a *for* loop.
    Print the song titles that have an even number of letters in the song name.
    At the end of the loop, print "Play it again!"

9. The Fibonacci sequence is a well-known series where a number is the sum of the two numbers preceding it. For example: 8 is the sum of $3 + 5$.

    ```
    fibonacci = [0, 1, 1, 2, 3, 5, 8, 13]
    ```

    a. Append the next two values in the Fibonacci series to the list.
    b. Print your Fibonacci list to confirm the values.

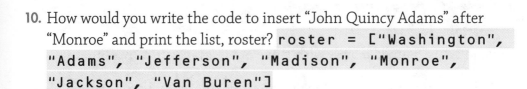

10. How would you write the code to insert "John Quincy Adams" after "Monroe" and print the list, roster? `roster = ["Washington", "Adams", "Jefferson", "Madison", "Monroe", "Jackson", "Van Buren"]`

Use this list for the following three questions. How would you write the following lines of code? Remember to test your code in Python to confirm your answer.

```
pets = ["dog", "cat", "bird", "turtle",
"horse", "fish", "snake"]
```

11. Write the line of code to remove "horse" from the list of pets.

12. Write the code to remove the current 4th element from the list.

13. Write the code to delete "snake" from the list.

Use the following list for questions 14-18.

14. Write the code to find and print the largest number in the list *weights*?

```
weights = [2, 4, 6, 7.5, 9.8, 42, 19]
```

What is produced after each of the following blocks of code?

```
weights = [2, 4, 6, 7.5, 9.8, 42, 19]
```

15. `print(sum(weights))`

16. `print(sum(weights) * 2)`

17. `print(sum(weights) / 2)`

18. `print(sum(weights) - 2)`

19. What is printed after the following lines of code?

```
nums = [42, 256, 1023]
print(nums * 3)
```

Flashcard App

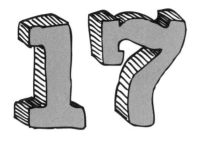

Repetitive Statements: while Loops

MUST ⚡ KNOW

 Repetitive statements are commonly called loops.

 Code is repeated for each iteration of the loop.

 while loops repeat until a condition is met.

> Our third type of programming statement is repetitive.
> Our third type of programming statement is repetitive.
> Our third type of programming statement is repetitive.
>
> (Get it? Eye roll accepted as confirmation.)

Repetitive statements are also referred to as **iterative statements** or **loops**. That is because lines of code that are associated with these statements repeat as many times as specified. There are several benefits of loops including that the code will be shorter because we can avoid duplicating lines of code. This also makes the code more readable and easier to understand. Also, if we need to correct an error or make an update, we only have to do this in one place. There are two types of loops we will discuss: *while* loops and *for* loops.

while Loops

These loops start with the keyword `while` and have a condition associated with them. The loop will repeat while the condition is true. The condition is set up the same way we set them up with *if* statements. Python also uses the colon, **:**, punctuation after the condition.

```
while (count < 10):
```

As long as a variable *count* is less than 10, any code associated with this *while* loop will continue to execute. We call *count* our iteration variable. Its value will be tested with each new pass or iteration through our loop.

When you press the *Enter* key after the colon, Python will automatically indent for you. Just as with *if* statements, any code associated with our *while* loop must be indented under it. The loop ends when the indentation is moved back a level.

> **BTW**
>
> *Python does not require parentheses around the condition, but it is okay to have them. The parentheses easily identify the condition. Other programming languages do require parentheses for while loop conditions, so using them now can help you transition to other languages in the future.*

```
while (count < 10):
    print ("count is: ", count)
    count = count + 2
```
Indentation is moved back and is even with while.
```
print("The loop is finished. ")
```

A common use of the *while* loop is to prompt a user or player for input. Using the **input()** command (see Chapter 12), we can prompt the user for data and ask them to type something else when they are finished. Our *while* loop will run until the user indicates they are finished.

- In lines 1 and 2 below, we declare the variables *counter* and *sumTemp* and initialize them to 0.

- Line 3 prompts users to key in temperature values or "stop" when they are done. The backslash character,\, indicates the line of code continues on the next line.

- Line 4 sets up our *while* loop to keep going until the user types "stop".

- For each temperature value the user types, line 5 casts it to be an integer. Remember all data coming in from the keyboard is a string datatype in Python.

- In line 6, we add our new temperature value to the existing total and store it back into the variable **sumTemp**.

- The counter variable is tracking how many values the user types in, so one more is added to it.

- We then prompt the user for another value or the word "stop".

- Lines 4–8 will keep repeating until the user types in "stop".

- Then line 9 prints out how many values were entered and our program ends.

```
1 counter = 0
2 sumTemp = 0
3 temp = input("Type in the temperatures. Type \
  'stop' when finished: ")
4 while(temp != "stop"):
5     temp = int(temp)
6     sumTemp = sumTemp + temp
7     counter = counter + 1
8     temp = input("Type another temperature or \
      'stop' when finished: ")
9 print("The average temperature value ",
  (sumTemp / counter))
```

while Loops: What Can Go Wrong?

A key factor with the condition in our *while* loop is that the condition must be able to become false. Somewhere in the block of code that executes while the condition is true, the value or values being tested must change so the condition can become false.

```
while (x < 10):
    print ("x is: ", x)
    x = x + 2
```

In the body of this loop, the value of x is increased by 2 each iteration. The variable *x* will eventually equal or be greater than 10, which will stop the loop.

If we did not have this, we would end up with an *infinite* loop. With an infinite loop, the condition never has a chance to change to false, so it continually repeats. Eventually, your computer's resources are used up and it crashes. A restart of your computer will free up the resources, but be sure to fix the loop before running it again!

What could we do to correct this infinite loop?

```
while (inning > 0):
    print ("Play ball!")
```

No matter how many innings are played, we never update our variable.

If we add a line of code to subtract 1 from the variable *inning* each iteration, the loop condition will eventually become 0, and the loop will end (and the game will be over!).

```
while (inning > 0):
    print ("Play ball!")
    # New line of code to ensure our loop ends
    inning = inning − 1
```

Sometimes, you can get lucky and use your keyboard keys to stop the infinite loop before it ties up all the computer's resources. For PCs and Macs, the *ctrl* + *c* keys will halt the program that is running.

while Loops: What Else Could Go Wrong?

If we are not careful with how we set up our condition, it is possible that our loop will never execute. These are called **Zero-trip Loops**. Here is an example of one.

```
x = 10
while (x < 10):
    print ("x = ", x)
```

What is printed after this loop is executed? Nothing prints because the loop condition is false the very first time it is tested. *x* has a value of 10 and we only enter the loop when *x* is less than 10. Oops! Zero-trip loop.

What happens if we change the condition to be less than or equal to 10?

```
x = 10
while (x <= 10):
    print("x = ", x)
```

Did you see that we now have an infinite loop? We need to change the iteration variable *x* to change with each pass through the loop. Will this next example work?

```
x = 0
while (x <= 10):
    print("x = ", x)
    x = x + 5
```

Yes! This one will work correctly. Our loop will execute three times.

- The first time, $x = 0$.

- The second time, $x = 5$.

- The third time, $x = 10$.

- The fourth iteration, $x = 15$, and the condition is false so the loop ends.

while Loops: Stopping in the Middle of an Iteration

Sometimes, we may need a way to end a *while* loop once an event occurs. We still have our condition to test at the start of each iteration of the loop. However, if an event occurs that causes us to not need to continue the loop, we can *break* out of it. As soon as *break* is used, no other lines of code in the loop are executed. The loop ends, and the program executes the next line of code after the loop or ends the program if there are no other lines of code.

In this loop, if we find an odd number by using our modulus math function (see Chapter 10), then we want to end the loop, even if *x* is still less than 10.

```
while (x < 10):
        if (x % 2 == 1):     # % provides the remainder.
                break
        print ("x = ", x)
        x = x + 2
```

The *break* command exits the loop. As soon as our *if* condition is true, *break* is executed, and no other lines of code inside the `while (x < 10):` loop are run. The program end since there are no other lines of code after the while loop.

Sometimes programmers will intentionally set up an infinite loop. They then use the *break* statement to exit the loop. In this example, you would need to be sure that the variable *gpa* would hold the string "stop" at some point.

```
while(True):
        gpa = input("Enter the grade point \
        average or 'stop' when finished: ")
        if (gpa == "stop"):
                break
        # process gpa
```

while Loops: Continuing in the Middle of an Iteration

Sometimes, we may need a way to end an iteration of a *while* loop when an event occurs without ending the loop. We still have our condition to test at the start of each iteration of the loop. However, if an event occurs that causes us to not need to process a data value, we can skip the rest of this iteration and begin the next iteration of the loop with the next data value. The *continue* command provides this functionality.

In this example, if we find an odd number by using our modulus math function, then we want to skip processing this value but stay in the loop until *x* is greater than or equal to 10. The modulus command % is used to test if a number is odd. When the remainder is 1 after dividing by 2, then a number is an odd number. If it is odd, one is added to the variable *x*, and then the *continue* command is executed. The program then moves back to the top of the loop to process the next iteration.

```
while (x < 10):
    if (x % 2 == 1):
        x = x + 1
        continue
    print ("x = ", x)
    x = x + 2
```

The *continue* command keeps us in the loop and skips the rest of the code with the current iteration. We move back to the top of our *while* loop to test the condition again. We will only leave the loop when the (x < 10) condition becomes false.

 IRL Some programmers refuse to use the break and continue commands. They are reminiscent of an old *go to* statement that could result in what is called "spaghetti code"!

REVIEW QUESTIONS

1. What causes an infinite loop?

2. When will an infinite loop end?

3. What punctuation is at the end of a *while* loop?

4. How do you let Python know that code does not belong in the while loop?

5. How would you change the following code so it will not execute infinitely?

```
while (score < 25):
    print("Serve the ball! ")
```

6. What has been printed after two passes through the following loop?

```
lives = 11
while (lives < = 10):
    lives = lives - 1
    print ("Lives remaining: ", lives)
print("Game over!")
```

7. How would you change the code to ensure the loop executes?

8. Set up a *while* loop to repeat four times.

   Ask the user for a type of animal they have as a pet, such as dog, cat, fish, and so on.

   If the pet is a gerbil, then break out of the loop.

9. Set up a *while* loop to run 5 times.

   Print the number of each iteration starting with 5.

   Decrease the number to print by 1 each iteration.

   After the *while* loop finishes, print the word "Blastoff!"

10. Define a *while* loop to run while a number is less than zero.
    Print the even numbers.
    Add one to the iteration variable.
    Print that the loop has completed its processing.

11. Write a while loop to repeat as many times as you have TV channels.
    If the program is "music channel", then continue.
    Otherwise, print the channel number.

12. Write a while loop to ask the user for input until they enter "done".
    Count the number of entries and print it after the loop ends.

Flashcard App

Repetitive Statements: for Loops

MUST KNOW

⚡ The *for* loop is another way to repeat code a set number of times.

⚡ Python handles when to end processing for a *for* loop, so there is no possibility of having an infinite loop.

⚡ The order for *for* and *in* is: *for* variable *in* data. *for* and *in* are reserved words and must be used in those positions.

⚡ The variable takes on the next value in the dataset with each iteration of the loop.

Our third type of programming statement is repetitive.
Our third type of programming statement is repetitive.
Our third type of programming statement is repetitive.

(Still get it? Definitely expect the eye roll this time!)

e are back with a different type of loop: *for* loops. This is the second type of loop we will cover. Any code that is associated with a *for* loop will repeat as many times as specified. Python keeps up with the number of times the loop should run and stops the loop when it is finished. This is called **traversing**. It travels across each element in the dataset and stops when it reaches the end.

The format to use with a *for* loop is:

```
for variable in data:
```

- *for* and *in* are reserved words in Python and are part of the *for* loop structure.

- The variable is called the *iteration* variable.

- The programmer decides what to call the iteration variable.

- As usual, make it descriptive, such as: *for* name *in* roster.

- The data could be a string, list, or file. The loop will repeat for each letter in the string, item in the list, or line in the file.

- The statement ends with a colon.

There is not a condition to evaluate with each iteration of a *for* loop like a *while* loop has. It runs for each item in the dataset and automatically then stops the loop. The program continues with the line of code after the loop or ends the program if there are no other lines of code.

BTW

for *loops are considered to be* **definite loops,** *because they run a specific number of times based on the data. A* **while** *loop is an* **indefinite loop,** *because it is not always known how long the condition will remain true and the loop will execute.*

BTW

You do not have to worry about infinite loops with a for loop. It cannot happen.

Just like our *while* loops, any code that needs to run with each iteration of the loop must be indented under the *for* statement. Also like the *while* loops and *if* statements, Python requires a colon after the *for* loop setup.

Strings and *for* Loops

We can use our *for* loop with strings. With strings, the *for* loop iterates through each character in the string. This example searches for the number of times a lowercase *o* appears in a string.

```
vowelO = 0
message = "Hello, World!"
for letter in message:
        if (letter == "o"):
                vowelO = vowelO + 1
        print(letter)
print("The letter 'o' appeared", vowelO, \
"times")
```

Note that:

- The iteration variable is *letter*. It first takes on the value *H*.

- The selection statement checks to see if it is a lowercase *o*. If it is, a counter is increased by 1. The value in the variable letter is printed.

- The program moves back to the beginning of the *for* loop and the iteration variable holds the next letter, *e*.

- The *if* statement checks to see if it is the letter *o*. Since it is not, the code moves on to print this letter.

- The program moves back to the start of the *for* loop and the variable letter now holds the next character in our string, a lowercase *l*.

Processing continues through each character in the string, including the exclamation point. Once there are no more characters in the string, the *for* loop ends and processing continues with any code after the *for* loop. In this example, we then print how many times the letter appeared in the string. Remember to use the \ continuation character if a line of code wraps to the next line.

for Loops and Lists

In this example, we first create a list of various types of fruit. (See Chapter 16 for more information about lists.) This example also uses the built-in method: `startswith()`. We saw `startswith()` earlier in Chapter 11 on strings. As you may guess, it checks to see if the first character in a data value is the same as the one inside the parentheses. Our example uses `startswith("b")`. Notice the format is:

```
variableName.startswith()
```

This method is associated with a variable. That's why the format includes a variable or list name + dot + the method name with parentheses and any values in the parentheses. Methods are special types of functions that are tied to an object, such as a variable or list.

Our object here is a list named fruit. If we have a list of several types of fruit, we can iterate through it with the *for* loop.

```
fruit = ["strawberry", "blueberry", "banana",
         "grapes", "apple", "orange"]
for food in fruit:
    if (food.startswith("b")):
        print(food)
```

With each iteration, the variable *food* takes on the value of the next fruit in our list. During the first iteration, the variable *food* contains the word "strawberry". It does not start with the letter *b*, so the condition is false and it is not printed. That is the end of processing the element "strawberry".

Next, the variable *food* takes on the value "blueberry". It does start with a *b*, so the condition is true and the contents of the variable *food* are printed. This value is currently "blueberry".

food then holds the value "banana". It does start with a *b*, so the condition is true and the contents of the variable *food* are printed. This value is currently "banana".

The loop continues with the values "grapes", "apple", and "orange", one at a time. After "orange" is processed, the loop ends without us having to tell it to stop.

You can use a *for* loop or a *while* loop to do the same processing. However, when you have a set number of data values to process, a *for* loop is the way to go. You will need additional lines of code with a *while* loop to keep up with iterations to avoid an infinite loop.

Here is the equivalent *while* loop to process the list of fruits.

```
fruit = ["strawberry", "blueberry", "banana",
        "grapes", "apple", "orange"]
count = 0        # A variable to keep up with the number of
                 items to process
while (count < len(fruit)):
    if (fruit[count].startswith("b")):
        print(fruit[count])
    count = count + 1
```

Notice the condition in the *while* loop. We are using the built-in function `len()` so we don't have to count how many elements are in our list. However, our condition has to be less than the length of the list. If we had less than or equal to, <=, we would get an index-out-of-range error. We do not have to worry about this error with a *for* loop.

BTW

*It is a valid programming structure to have a loop within a loop. This is called **nesting loops**. This is possible with both **while** and **for** loops. You will need a setup like this when working with a table or matrix.*

Also notice how we have to reference each item in our list of fruit. We have to provide the list name, and, using brackets, we also provide the index position of an element. We use our counter variable for the index position. In the *for* loop, the iteration variable takes on each value automatically, so we do not have to provide the index position for the list elements.

Both *while* loops and *for* loops are powerful and frequently used in programs. Each has uses where one is the better choice over the other.

REVIEW QUESTIONS

1. How does Python know which lines of code are associated with a *for* loop?

2. What punctuation goes at the end of the *for* loop statement?

3. What is the value of the iteration variable *counter* in each iteration?
```
for counter in [5, 4, 3, 2, 1]:
    print(counter)
print("Blastoff!")
```

4. What do the last two iterations display?
```
roster = ["Michael", "Kathleen", "Elyse",
    "Richard"]
locker = 101
for name in roster:
    print("Locker#: ", locker, name)
    locker = locker + 1
```

5. Write a *for* loop to process the string "Mississippi".
   Count how many times the letter *s* appears in the string.
   Print the total count after the loop finishes.

Functions

MUST ⚡ KNOW

⚡ Programming languages include built-in functions, which are prewritten, pretested blocks of code available for use.

⚡ We can also define our own functions in Python.

⚡ Arguments are used to send data to a function while parameters are local variables that use the data from the arguments inside the function.

⚡ The *return* statement will immediately exit a function and can include data to send back to the calling program.

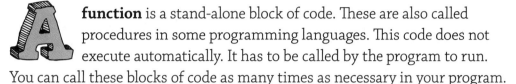 **function** is a stand-alone block of code. These are also called procedures in some programming languages. This code does not execute automatically. It has to be called by the program to run. You can call these blocks of code as many times as necessary in your program.

When you are designing your program, anytime you see a need for the same code more than once at different places in your program, that is a sign that you should create a function. If you are writing the program and find yourself duplicating code, that's what a function was made to replace.

The benefits include shorter and more readable code. Plus, if you make a mistake or need to update the code, you only have to change it in one place. These are huge benefits! (Loops has the same benefits.)

Built-In Functions

We have used built-in functions several times in earlier chapters starting with the **print()** function. Built-in functions *cannot* be changed. They were written as part of the programming language and are automatically available. Built-in functions make up algorithms that many programmers need. It made more sense for the developers of the programming language to include these working modules for everyone. They save a lot of time, because each programmer does not have to develop his or her own code to address the same need.

As an example, let's consider the **print()** function again. It is a reserved word in Python and changes color as a visual clue that it is reserved when used in the program. Functions also always need to have parentheses. We do not see the code for the **print()** function, but we can use it as many times as we need to in our program. This is one of the built-in functions that is included with Python. We have also used the **int()**, **float()**, **str()**, and **input()** built-in functions in earlier chapters. When Python sees a function name it recognizes, it pauses the program, goes to find the code for the function, executes it, then returns to the point in the program where it paused to resume processing. This happens so quickly that it is imperceptible to us.

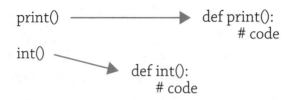

Calling a function sends the program to find where it is defined to execute the code.

There are many built-in functions that come with each programming language. You need to check the official documentation for the programming language you are using to find out what built-in functions are available to you and how to use them. Go to the official Python documentation site to view the list of built-in functions available: docs.python.org/3/library/functions.html.

Functions You Create

In addition to having built-in functions available for use, programmers can also write their own customized functions. Remember, if you find yourself duplicating code, you should use a function. Functions we create need to be defined before we can use them in our program. Therefore, common practice is to define them at the top of our program right after our header comments.

```
# name
# date
# brief description of program
# define functions
```

In Python, use the *def* keyword to define a function, followed by a name for the function that we get to choose, parentheses, and a colon. Then, indent code that belongs to the function under it.

```
def functionName ( ):
```

It is a good programming practice to give a function a name that describes what it does, just as we do with variables. This makes it easier to understand your code. If you combine words in your function name, start with a lowercase letter and then start each successive word with a capital letter, e.g., "camelCase".

All functions, built-in and those written by us, must have parentheses.

Python uses the colon, :, to indicate the end of the *def* statement. When you press the *Enter* key, Python will automatically indent the next line.

```
def calcAvg():          # Function to calculate the average
```

Indentation with functions is once again very important in Python. All of the code that belongs to a function is indented one level underneath it. When the function is finished, the next line of code is unindented back to the left margin.

Let's add some code in our function to calculate an average.

```
def calcAvg():          # Use parentheses so the correct order
                        # of operations will be used.

avg = (12345 + 6789 + 54321) / 3

print("The average is: ", avg)
```

A function will not run until it is called. It sits there where it was defined, waiting to be put into the game. We call a function by typing its name and the parentheses. The program pauses, goes and finds the code for the function, runs that code, then returns to the place the function was called and continues processing.

```
calcAvg()    # Call to the function calcAvg()
```

Notice that you do not use the colon punctuation when you call the function. However, you do need to include the parentheses.

Once you have a function coded and tested, you can trust that it works and leave it alone! This is the same way built-in functions work. We do not need to see the code or understand it. We just know that it "works as advertised" in the documentation. Functions, both built-in and customized, can be called as many times as needed in a program. There is also no limit on the number of functions you can define in your program.

> **BTW**
>
> Once you have created a function, do not reuse the same name you gave the function as a variable name!

Parameters and Arguments

Sometimes, we want to send data to a function. We do this when we use the *print()* function by including what we want to have printed in the parentheses. We can print a variable, an expression that must be calculated before printing, or a text field.

```
# Variable holding the current temperature
temp = 82
# Print a string.
print("Hello, world!")
# Print a variable.
print("The current temperature is ", temp)
# Calculate, then print an expression.
print("Degrees above freezing: ", temp – 32)
```

The data that we send to functions are called **arguments**. These values can change each time the function is called, which is one reason they are so powerful and useful! In the above examples:

```
"Hello, world!"
```
 is the argument

```
"The current temperature is"
```
 and `temp` are both arguments separated by a comma

`"Degrees above freezing:"` and `temp — 32` are both arguments separated by a comma

A **parameter** is used in the function as a holding place for the value that is sent to it as an argument.

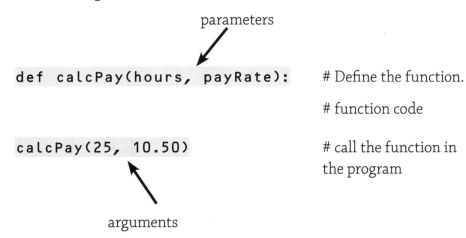

parameters

```
def calcPay(hours, payRate):     # Define the function.

                                 # function code

calcPay(25, 10.50)               # call the function in
                                   the program
```

arguments

Not all functions have parameters, but every function does need the parentheses. Even if the function does not have parameters, you must use the parentheses when you define and call the function. You specify any parameters when you define a function. For example, the function "score" has two parameters.

```
def score (win, lose):     # Lines of code not included for
                             clarity
```

When we call the score function, we must pass it two arguments. This example calls the function with two variables as the arguments.

```
score(gameWin, gameLose)
```

We could also call the function using two numbers as the arguments.

```
score(42, 20)
```

As you might guess, we can also call the function with a combination of numbers or variables.

```
score(22, visitorScore)
```

```
score(homeScore, 24)
```

Be sure to pass the arguments in the correct order. Our code would produce inaccurate results if we called score with:

```
score(gameLose, gameWin)
```

Notice that the names for the arguments and parameters are not the same in the example above. While you can name them the same, it makes it much harder to troubleshoot errors if you do. Be creative and use different names for the parameters and arguments!

Many programming languages are very particular about the argument and the parameter datatypes matching. Python is flexible in this aspect.

```
team1 = 11
team2 = 7
score(team1, team2)

score(55, 44)

score("win", 42)
```

These are all valid calls to the score function. Python automatically converts the datatypes and accepts the string argument passed to it. Most programming languages would throw an error in this case. Therefore, it is a good idea to get into the habit now of passing arguments of the same datatype as the parameters.

If a function does not have parameters, do not provide any arguments when you call it. Similarly, if a function does have parameters, you must provide the arguments when you call it. Python will display an error message if we call score with only one argument or no arguments.

```
score(5)
Traceback (most recent call last):
    File "<pyshell#29>", line 1, in <module>
```

```
      score(5)
TypeError: score() missing 1 required positional
   argument: 'lose'
```

```
score()
Traceback (most recent call last):
  File "<pyshell#30>", line 1, in <module>
    score()
TypeError: score() missing 2 required positional
   arguments: 'win' and 'lose'
```

You can also use a call to another function as one of your arguments. This example calls the function *highScore*. One of the arguments is a call to our *score* function and includes two arguments which *score* needs. The call to highScore will be paused while the program runs the code for score(Win, Loss). The outcome of that function call will be used as one argument. The other argument for highScore() is a variable named currentTopScore.

```
highScore(score(Win, Loss), currentTopScore)
```

You can call a function from a different function as long as you pass it any needed arguments.

Global and Local Variables

Variables have a scope or area in a program where they are recognized or known to the program. When we define variables at the top of our program, this makes them global. A **global** variable is available and known to the entire program.

When a variable is created in a function, then it is **local** to that function only. If you try to reference it outside of the function, you will see an error message similar to the one below. In this error message, the variable name, *message*, was used outside of the function where it was defined.

```
NameError: name 'message' is not defined
```

If you want to reference a global variable in a function, you need to tell Python. We do this using the *global* keyword and the name of the variable already defined globally that we want to use. We place this line of code right after the function definition so the global variable will be available before we try to use it.

```
def myFunction():
    # The function uses the global variable
    named counter.
    global counter
    counter = counter + 1
```

The variable that you are using globally in a function must have already been defined. If you forget to include a global variable in a function, Python will instead create a *local* variable with the same name when you use it in the function. This is not good because now you have two variables with the same name, one global and one local. This makes debugging difficult because you likely do not realize you have two different variables. You most likely think you are using the global one only, and your results are probably not accurate for some of your test cases.

```
def myFunction():
    # Python creates a local variable named
    counter.
    counter = counter + 1
```

In the example below, we have a global variable *name* with the value "myself". In function `func1()`, we have a local variable *name* with the value "me". Function `func2()` uses the global variable name through the `global` command.

```
def func1():
  name = "me"
  # Updates the local variable
  name = "I"
def func2():
  global name
  # Updates the global variable
  name = "me myself and I"
# Main program
name = "myself" # initialize global variable
func1()
func2()
print(name)
# The output printed is for the global
variable
me myself and I
```

**Use of a global and local variable,
both called *name* in functions**

Note that if you are only using and not changing a global variable's value in a function, then a local variable will *not* be created if you do not declare it as global. A local variable is only created for the variable on the left-hand side when an assignment statement is executed. In this example, a new local variable, *timer*, will be created. The global variables for variables *time* and *delay* will be used without having to define them as global in the function since they are not changing.

```
def howLong():
    timer = time + delay
    print("Total time:", timer)
time = 55
delay = 4
howLong()
```

The output will be:

```
Total time: 59
```

Functions: The *return* Statement

Functions have an optional feature called a *return* statement. The *return* statement has two uses. One purpose is to end a function before the code ends, similarly to how the *break* statement works with loops. The other use is to return a value back to the calling program.

For example, we can define a function to ensure all elements in a list are even. If we find an odd number, we want to exit our function. We will use modulus math to see if a number is even. If it is odd, we will return to the calling program immediately.

```
1    # define function
2    def onlyEven (numbers):
3        total = 0
4        for num in numbers:
5            if (num% 2 ! = 0):
6                # Returns to the calling program
                 if an odd number is found.
7                return("Found an odd number")
```

```
8          else:
9              total = total + num
10         print ("All even numbers")
11         # Returns the sum of all the numbers
           # only if all numbers are even.
12         return total
13
14     # Define list.
15     nums = [2, 4, 6, 8, 11, 12, 14, 16,
       18, 20]
16
17     # Main program
18     # Call the function onlyEven
19     print(onlyEven(nums))
```

Our program will call the function **onlyEven()** passing the list named *nums* as an argument. With this list, there is an odd number, so the program will return the message "Found an odd number" and immediately return back to the program that called it, which will print the message. The program is then finished.

If all the numbers are even, then after the entire list is processed, the message "All even numbers" is printed and just the sum of all the numbers in the list is returned to the calling program, which then prints the sum.

Functions can be used to calculate and return a value as part of an expression. In other words, they can be stacked together. It can get confusing quickly, and it is just as correct to break each step out and store the intermediate steps into variables.

```
1      def circumference (radius):
2          circ = 2 * 3.14 * r
3          return circ
4
```

```
5    def areaCircle(radius):
6        area = 3.14 * radius * radius
7        return area
8
9    # Print the text and the variable rad
10   # Then call the function circumference.
11   # The print statement is paused while the
     function
12   # is processing.
13   # The value calculated in the function
     will be
14   # returned and printed.
15   rad = 5
16   print("The circumference of the circle
         with a radius of",
17         rad, "is", circumference(rad))
18
19   # Example of calculating the area of a
     circle
20   # using intermediate steps
21   area = areaCircle(rad)
22   print ("The area of a circle with a
             radius of",
23           rad, "is", area)
```

Functions are very powerful features of programs. We can use existing functions or write our own customized ones and use both types as often as needed in our code. Arguments send data to our functions, and existing program-wide variables can be used with the global command. Functions can also send data back to the calling program if needed. *Remember, a function will not run until it is called,* which is often confusing for new programmers.

REVIEW QUESTIONS

1. How can programmers tell a word is reserved if they are not familiar with it?

2. Can a programmer change a built-in function?

3. Can a variable have the same name as a built-in function?

4. What keyword is used to start creating a function?

5. Is any punctuation used when creating a function?

6. How does Python know when a function definition is complete?

7. How do you call a function?

8. Define a function to calculate the average temperature.
   Use at least four numbers in your calculation.
   Print a message that: "The average temperature was " and your
   calculated value.
   Then call your function to test that it works correctly.

9. How does a parameter differ from an argument?

10. Are parentheses required with functions?

11. What punctuation is used to separate arguments and parameters?

12. Define a function to calculate the average of two values.
    There are two parameters.
    Calculate the average using the values passed to the two parameters.
    Print the output.

13. Is a variable defined in a function global or local?

14. What is the scope of a global variable?

15. How do you include a global variable in a function?

16. Create a function named *myPets* and add a global variable for *currentPet*.

17. Define a function with two parameters.
   Use an *if* statement to determine which number is larger.
   Return the larger number.

20 Libraries and APIs

T here are prewritten programs available in Python, plus external libraries of code that have been shared for anyone to use, as well as APIs to allow our programs to communicate with external applications. There's no reason to rewrite code that has already been prewritten and tested, so always check for these.

View Available Modules, Keywords, Symbols, and Topics

First, to view all the modules the Python provides, so that you do not rewrite something that is already available to use, you can use the Python IDLE that is downloaded to your computer. From the prompt in the shell, type:

```
>>>help()
```

Information is displayed about how to navigate through `help()`. From the `help>` prompt, type:

```
help> modules
```

A list of all the modules available in Python version 3 is displayed. You can then enter the name of any module you need to see detailed information about.

If you already know the name of a module you need details about, from the shell prompt, you can type:

```
>>>help(module_name)
```

This same process can be used to find out detailed information about all:

Keywords

Symbols

Topics

```
>>>help()
help> keywords
help> symbols
help> topics
```

If you already know the name of the keyword, symbol, or topic, you can type the name of it in the parentheses (the argument) of the **help()** function. You need to enclose the name in quotation marks.

```
>>>help("keyword_name")
>>>help("symbol")
>>>help("topic")
```

Another way to check the available files in a module is to use the directory function: **dir()**. First, import the module. You can then pass the name of a module with **dir()** to see all the filenames in a module.

```
>>> import random
>>> dir(random)
```

The output will be all the names of the files you get when you import *random*. You can also use **dir()** without including an argument. In this case, all the names you have currently available in your program are listed.

To see the list of built-in functions and variables, you can use:

```
>>> import builtins
>>> dir(builtins)
```

Whether you are using an online editor or the downloaded version on your computer, you can always check the official Python documentation to see what modules, keywords, symbols, and topics are available along with a description of each.

- The link for the official documentation is https://docs.python.org/3/.

- It will open to the most recent released version of the software.

- You can also see the documentation for prior versions on the left-hand side, if needed.

Modules Available with Python

Like the built-in functions that we have talked about with lists and strings, there are many modules available in Python, plus modules that other people have written that are available for use. The functions that you write can also be stored in a file and shared with others to use.

Modules are files that include code that can be imported into your programs. The files generally contain multiple functions that can then be used in your program. You have to import modules before you can call them in your program. Generally accepted programming practice is to place import statements at the top of your program, just after the header comments. One example is a random number generator. These are often needed in programs.

```
# author name
# date created/last modified
# brief description of program
import random
```

To use a function in the random module, you have to type:

```
the module name + . + the file name.
```

For example, to use the *randint* function to generate a random integer between 1 and 100, use:

```
random.randint(1,100)
```

How to Find or Create Modules to Share

The Python Package Index (PyPI) lets anyone find available packages that have been developed and shared for all to use. There is an online User Guide to walk you through using the package index along with a frequently asked questions (FAQs) section, both of which are useful.

It also contains instructions for packaging code to share with others. There are tutorials to follow to do this. The most current information and list of available packages are on the website: https://pypi.org/.

Libraries and APIs

Similar to the built-in functions, there are times you may want to interface with a web-based application, such as a search engine or video site. Most of these sites provide code to use to integrate your site with theirs. Programmers need to understand what is included and how to use each one. The Application Programming Interface (API) provides this information for programmers. There are many sites that list commonly used Python APIs with links to the code you must include in your program to successfully interface with it. You can do an online search for Python APIs to find these.

> No review questions in this chapter. Let's jump right to the next chapter and get started on a few projects!

Flashcard App

21 Projects

MUST KNOW

 In this chapter, we're going to apply the **must know** concepts we've learned to five brand-new projects.

hroughout the book, we've written sections of code to learn new concepts and how to implement them in Python. You now have the fundamental skills to write programs, so let's create! Be aware that the margins in this book are smaller than what you'll have available for your programs. The examples here that spread code over multiple lines do not have to do that in the Python IDLE. When you do need to split the text inside a print() statement, use the backslash symbol \ to tell Python the text is continued on the next line. Otherwise, you will get an error. Similarly, when you need to wrap other lines of code to a new line, be sure to split at a natural breaking point, such as after a comma or parenthesis.

Project 1: Crazy Talk!

This is along the lines of the Mad Libs game. We want to ask a player for certain types of words, and then we'll produce funny sentences as output using their words. We will use our Software Development Life Cycle to plan our project. We need to ensure we understand how our game will work before we start to code.

We need to know how many words we will prompt the player for and what type of words, such as nouns or adjectives. As the client requesting this game, I would like the player to provide two nouns, two adjectives, and a verb. These will be filled into certain locations in a sentence. We know for each round of the game, we'll need to prompt the user for these. Let's create a flowchart as we go through our design in order, to diagram our algorithm.

Step 1   Let's add our starting point and an input box.

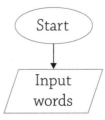

Step 2   Next, we'll need to construct a sentence with some standard words and places to fill in with the player's words. A list would be a good way to

hold different phrases to use in our sentence. We'll need to preload these so our player won't have to provide everything. It wouldn't have the element of surprise either. Let's add a process box to our flowchart to set up our initial words and lists. I would do this before asking for input, so we'll put this box right after *Start* and move input words after we initialize everything.

Initialize
variables
and lists

Step 3   We should have all of the words we need, so now we need to form the sentences. We want each to be different, and the sillier the better. A good way to do this would be to randomly choose an element from our list of sentence phrases each time we need one and print it. We'll need to add a process box to our flowchart to generate the sentence from the list of words. We can also add one to print the result.

Create
sentence

Print
sentence

Step 4   We do want our players to be able to create more crazy talk, so we should set up a way to ask them if they want to play again.

Play
again?

End

Here is the finished flowchart for our algorithm.

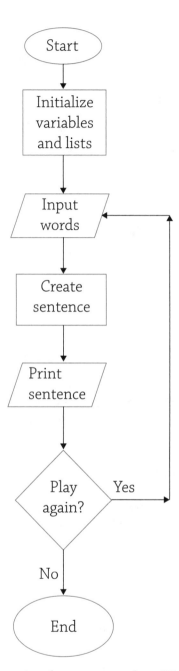

Start

Initialize
variables
and lists

Input
words

Create
sentence

Print
sentence

Play
again?

Yes

No

End

Now let's write the code to implement our plan. We can start by setting up the section of code to start the game and ask the player for the words.

We will need five variables to hold the different words. We will need descriptive variable names to keep up with each one. I will call mine noun1, noun2, adj1, adj2, and verb so I don't confuse the word types. To start the program, I will place comments at the top with name, date created, and a description of the program and then define and initialize the variables.

```
# Name
# Date created
# Program to create silly sentences with words provided by the player
noun1 = ""
noun2 = ""
adj1 = ""
adj2 = ""
verb = ""
```

Since we want to randomly pick values out of the sentence fragments, we'll need to import the *random* library when we're writing our code. We'll add that next.

```
import random
```

We should provide some instructions on how to play. We should display these each time a new game is started. Let's place them in a function so that we can call it when we want the instructions to display. This section of code should go near the top of our program, after the import statement. Remember the *newline* escape character is \n. I'm using it to help with formatting the instructions. Also, the \ is the continuation character needed when a line of code spans over multiple lines.

```
def instructions():
    print("Welcome to Crazy Talk, the game where \
        you help write the story. \nI will ask you \
        for a type of word, such as noun or verb.")
```

```
    print("I will then generate a sentence using \
        your words to see how crazy it is! \n")
```

Now, we can set up the sentence segments in lists.

```
startSent = ["The", "A", "One", "How", "Be",
             "If", "What", "Who", "When", "Where"]
  midSent = ["away from the", "out of the",
             "in the lake with the", "ran to",
             "swam from", ]
```

Now, we're ready to ask the user if they want to play our game:

```
print("Do you want to play a word game?")
play = input("Enter 'y' or 'n': ")
```

If the answer is "y", then we should print the instructions, so let's add a call to that function. It could stand alone with an *if* statement to check if the player typed in "y", but let's place it inside a loop. Now we can set up a **while** loop to run if the user wants to play.

```
while (play == "y"):
   instructions()
   noun1 = input("Please type in a noun: ")
   adj1 = input("Now give me an adjective: ")
   verb = input("Now I need a verb: ")
   noun2 = input("Please provide another noun: ")
   adj2 = input("And I need one more adjective: ")
```

Now we need to set up the sentence by selecting random sections from our sentence lists and building our sentence with the user's words. This is still under the `while` loop. There is a lot going on in this print statement! Let's break it down. First, we are randomly selecting an item from our *startSent* list. Our list starts at index position 0 and instead of counting the number of items and hardcoding the length, I used the `len()` function to determine the length of the list and then subtracted one to get the last index position. Then, if I add more items to the list, I won't have to remember to update the number of items in the `random.randint()` statement. I used the same structure for the random selection of the mid-sentence phrase. These may look a little intimidating, but you have all the knowledge needed to use them. The rest of the items in the print statement are our variables holding the words the user typed.

```
print(startSent[random.randint(0,len
    (startSent)-1)], adj2, noun1, verb,
midSent[random.randint(0, len(midSent)-1)], adj1,
    noun2, "!")
```

After we print the silly sentence, let's ask the user if they want to play another round.

```
print("Do you want to play again?")
play = input("Enter 'y' or 'n': ")
```

Finally, we need to thank the user for playing. This statement is outside of the `while` loop, so it is not indented and is flush with the left margin.

```
print("Thanks for playing!")
```

Here is our completed code:

```
# Name
# Date created
# Program to create silly sentences with words
# provided by the player

import random

# Define function to print instructions
def instructions():
    print("Welcome to Crazy Talk, the game where \
    you help write the story. \nI will ask you for \
    a type or word, such as noun or verb.")
    print("I will then generate a sentence using \
    your words to see how crazy it is! \n")

# Declare and initialize variables
noun1 = ""
noun2 = ""
adj1 = ""
adj2 = ""
verb = ""

startSent = ["The", "A", "One", "How", "Be",
    "If", "What", "Who", "When", "Where"]
midSent = ["away from the", "out of the",
    "in the lake with the", "on the bus",
    "in the car"]

print("Do you want to play a word game?")
    play = input("Enter 'y' or 'n': ")
```

```
while (play == "y"):
    instructions()
    noun1 = input("Please type in a noun: ")
    adj1 = input("Now give me an adjective: ")
    verb = input("Now I need a verb: ")
    noun2 = input("Please provide another noun: ")
    adj2 = input("And I need one more adjective: ")

    print(startSent[random.randint(0,
        len(startSent)-1)], adj2, noun1, verb,
        midSent[random.randint(0, len(midSent)-1)],
        adj1, noun2, "!")
    print("Do you want to play again?")
    play = input("Enter 'y' or 'n': ")


print("Thanks for playing!")
```

Be sure to test your code thoroughly. I always find typos in my own, and my code won't run until I fix them. Remember, there are multiple ways to write a correct program. Even if yours is not exactly like this one, it can still be correct! Find ways to enhance or improve your program. Make it more fun for the player. You can keep adding to the startSent and midSent lists to keep making funny sentences.

Project 2: Rock, Paper, Scissors

Most people have played rock, paper, scissors, whether it's to pass time or to decide who gets to do something like go first if they win or take out the trash if they lose. It is another game of chance that is fun to play and easy to program! Let's give it a whirl!

In our design phase, let's be sure we understand the rules of the game. After a countdown, the two players produce a symbol for either a rock (fist), paper (palm open facing down), or scissors (index and middle fingers straight, the rest tucked in.) The winner of a round is determined by:

- Rock smashes scissors.

- Paper covers rock.

- Scissors cut paper.

If both players make the same symbol, it's a tie.

Let's use pseudocode to design this solution. You can also make a flowchart if you prefer a diagram.

> Give the user instructions on what to enter for each choice.
>
> Pick a random option for the computer.
>
> Compare the user's choice to the computer's selection.
>
> If they are the same, print "tie!"
>
> If one choice is rock and the other is scissors, print "rock wins".
>
> If one choice is rock and the other is paper, print "paper wins".
>
> If one choice is paper and the other is scissors, print "scissors wins".
>
> Ask the player if they want to play again.

Here is a sample flowchart as well.

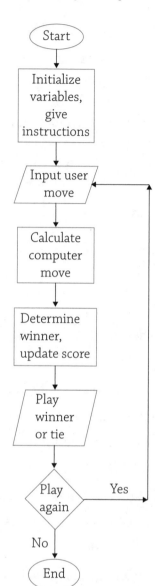

Let's begin coding now. As always, start with the comments at the top.

Name

Date

Rock, paper, scissors game: player vs. the computer

We will need to import the random module for this program too.

```
import random
```

We need to print the game instructions for the user. In project 1, the Crazy Talk program, we created a function for the instructions. This time, we'll just print them out at the beginning. We could have the user type in numbers for their choice, where 1 = rock, 2 = paper, 3 = scissors, but using the first letter of each word is easier to understand, so we'll go with that. The example below spreads the print() statement over multiple lines due to spacing. In your program, you'll need to either have the entire print() statement on one line or use the continuation character \ to continue to a new line.

```
print("Welcome to the Rock, Paper, Scissors \
   game!")
print("If you want to challenge the computer to a \
   game, then do the following:")
print("Enter an 'r' for rock, \n 'p' for paper or \
   \n 's' for scissors: ")
user = input()
```

Note that I could have used one `print()` statement and used escape characters to format it. We will need to generate a random number to represent the computer's choice.

```
computer = random.randint(1,3)
```

We need to convert the computer's choice to match what the player could type for the game to work. Otherwise, we'll be comparing a number to a letter, and they will never match! To keep our program uncluttered, let's make a function for this. Functions have to be defined before we can use them, so it needs to go at the top of our program, after the *import* statement. I'll name mine `convert()` since I am converting the computer's random number to an *r*, *p*, or *s*.

```
def convert():
  global computer
  if (computer == 1):
    computer = 'r'
  elif (computer == 2):
    computer = 'p'
  else:
    computer = 's'
```

We have to declare our variable *computer* to be a global variable because we are changing its value in our function from a number to a letter. We'll get an error if we don't declare it as global since our program is expecting it to already have a value stored in it before using it in the *if* statement's condition. Remember that when we forget to include a global variable, a local variable would be created. However, it would not be available to the rest of the program because its scope is only within this function. Therefore, our program could produce inaccurate and confusing results!

We could just as easily convert the user's response to a number. Remember, there's always more than one right way to correctly code a program. Don't forget to add a call to our `convert()` function in the program. Otherwise, it will never run.

Now we need to set up all of the comparisons using the *if/elif/else* structure and print out the results. I'm going to add the newline escape character to each print statement to make the output easier to read.

```
if (computer == user):
  print("\nIt's a tie!")
elif (computer == "r" and user == "s"):
  print("\nRock smashes scissors...the computer \
  wins!")
elif (computer == "r" and user == "p"):
  print("\nPaper covers rock...You win!")
elif (computer == "p" and user == "s"):
  print("\nScissors cut paper...You win!")
```

```
elif (computer == "s" and user == "r"):
   print("\nRock smashes scissors…You win!")
elif (computer == "p" and user == "r"):
   print("\nPaper covers rock…the computer wins!")
elif (computer == "s" and user == "p"):
   print("\nScissors cut paper…the computer wins!")
else:
   print("\nInvalid choice. You must choose "r", \
   "p", or "s")
```

We need to wrap this in a loop so that the user can play multiple times and decide when to stop. This also allows users who type in the wrong choice to try again without restarting the game. Let's set up a loop a different way this time. If we set our condition for a **while** loop to be *True*, it will be an infinite loop. Therefore, we can practice using our *break* statement to end the loop if an event occurs. Let's give the user additional instructions to type *e* to end the game. We'll need to add a new comparison to see if the user entered *e* and break out of the game if they did. Remember the *break* command causes the loop to end immediately. The program will continue with the first statement after the loop or end the program if there are no more lines of code to execute.

```
while (True):
   if (user == "e"):
      break
```

We also need to give the user another opportunity to enter their choice or end the game. The last statement in our **while** loop needs to be another **input()** statement. If they want to keep playing, then we also need to generate another move for the computer.

Let's add a way to keep track of the score if the user and computer played several rounds. This game plays quickly, so someone will likely play multiple times if they are just killing time.

We'll need a variable for the number of user wins and another one to track the computer wins. These should be initialized at the beginning of our program.

```
computerWins = 0
userWins = 0
```

Then, we'll need to update our code to add one to the correct score based on who wins a round in each of the *if/elif* conditions.

```
computerWins = computerWins + 1
```

or

```
userWins = userWins + 1
```

We could also write these as:

```
computerWins += 1
userWins += userWins
```

We should also print out the score at the end of each round.

```
print("\nScore: Player - ", userWins,
    "Computer - ", computerWins)
```

Let's add a little encouragement to keep playing by including who is winning as well as the number of wins each. This could be in our `while` loop, but I'm going to place it in a function along with the score to keep the code cleaner and call the function in the loop. This selection statement will be in the function.

```
if (computerWins == userWins):
    print("It's a tie! You need to keep playing to \
    see who wins! ")
```

```
elif (computerWins > userWins):
  print("The computer is winning! Try again to \
  beat the computer! ")
else:
  print("You are winning! Keep playing to \
  lengthen your lead on the computer!")
```

You can decide if you want there to be a limit on the number of plays, such as 21 rounds, or to just keep going until the user enters an *e*.

Don't forget to add comments to make the program easier to read and understand. Here's one solution for our Rock, Paper, Scissors game. The example below spreads the print() statements over multiple lines due to spacing. In your program, you should be able to fit it all on one line. Otherwise, remember to include the backslash continuation character \ to tell Python the line of code continues on the next line.

```
# Name
# Date
# Rock, paper, scissors game: player vs. computer

import random

# Function to convert the computer's random
# number to a letter
def convert():
  global computer
  if (computer == 1):
    computer = 'r'
  elif (computer == 2):
    computer = 'p'
  else:
    computer = 's'
```

```python
# track the score and total number of wins
def score():
  print("\nScore: Player - ", userWins,
  "Computer - ", computerWins)
  if (computerWins == userWins and computerWins >
  0):
    print("\nIt's a tie! You need to keep playing \
    to see who wins!")
  elif (computerWins > userWins):
    print("\nThe computer is winning! Try again to \
    beat the computer!")
  elif (computerWins < userWins):
    print("\nYou are winning! Keep playing to \
    increase your lead on the computer!")

computerWins = 0
userWins = 0

# Print instructions on how to play
print("Welcome to the Rock, Paper, Scissors \
  game!")
print("If you want to challenge the computer to a \
  game, then do the following:")
print("Enter an 'r' for rock, 'p' for paper or \
  's' for scissors or 'e' to end the game: ")
user = input()

# Generate computer's choice
computer = random.randint(1,3)

while (True):
  # Check if player wants to end the game
  if (user == "e"):
```

```
    print("Come back and play again soon!")
    break

# call function to convert computer number to
# letter
convert()


# Determine winner
if (computer == user):
    print("\nIt's a tie!")
elif (computer == "r" and user == "s"):
    computerWins = computerWins + 1
    print("\nRock smashes scissors...the computer \
    wins!")
elif (computer == "r" and user == "p"):
    userWins = userWins + 1
    print("\nPaper covers rock...You win!")
elif (computer == "p" and user == "s"):
    userWins = userWins + 1
    print("\nScissors cut paper...You win!")
elif (computer == "s" and user == "r"):
    userWins = userWins + 1
    print("\nRock smashes scissors...You win!")
elif (computer == "p" and user == "r"):
    computerWins = computerWins + 1
    print("\nPaper covers rock...the computer wins!")
elif (computer == "s" and user == "p"):
    computerWins = computerWins + 1
    print("\nScissors cut paper...the computer \
    wins!")
else:
    print("\nInvalid choice. You must choose 'r', \
    'p', 's', or 'e'")
```

```
# Print score
score()

# Play again?
print("\nIf you want to play again, \
  enter 'r', 'p', or 's', or 'e' to End the \
  game: ")
user = input()
computer = random.randint(1,3)
```

As always, remember to thoroughly test your code. Get a friend or family member to try it out after you get all the initial errors corrected. Your code will be better with someone else's input!

Project 3: Guess a Number

Our next project will be a guessing game. Did you know that you can guess a number between 1 and 100 in seven guesses or less? There is an algorithm, or set of steps, to follow for your guesses, and there are two conditions for the algorithm to work. First, the player who knows the number must provide feedback telling you if the number is higher or lower than your guess. The other condition applies when a program is searching a dataset for a specific value. For this algorithm to work, the dataset must be sorted.

This algorithm is called a **Binary Search**. It is a well-known and frequently used searching technique mainly because it is so efficient! The way it works is to always guess the number in the middle of the range. If our number range is 1–100, then our first guess will be 50. The person who knows the number will tell us if the actual number is higher or lower than our guess. If the actual number is higher than our guess, then we know it is between 51–100. We can throw away all the numbers from 1–50 because we know it cannot be any of those. We just eliminated half of our eligible numbers!

For our second guess, we select the halfway point between 51–100, so we guess 75. Again, we will receive feedback about whether the actual number is higher or lower than our guess. Once again, we can toss half of our possible numbers based on this information. We repeat the process of guessing the midpoint of the remaining pool of numbers and either guess the number or get additional feedback so we can remove half of the remaining numbers. If you don't have exactly a midpoint, you can guess either of the numbers that span the midpoint. For example, if you are down to guessing between 1–6, the midpoint could be 3 or 4. Pick either one of them as your guess, and based on the feedback, continue the algorithm.

You can now probably see why it is called a binary search. We bisect the available numbers with our guess and can throw away half of them with each round until we guess the number. With a pool of 100 numbers, we can guess the number in at most seven guesses, as long as we follow the algorithm. With a pool of 1,000 numbers, we can guess the number in at most ten guesses! It's a great way to amaze your friends until they begin to see the pattern you are using for guessing the numbers.

Let's code this guessing game using the binary search algorithm. To start, we'll need to give our players instructions on how to play our guessing game. They will have to guess a new number each time they are prompted. The program will provide the higher or lower information after each guess. Let's place this information in a function and call it when needed.

```
def instructions():
  print("Welcome to the Guessing Game!")
  print("I am thinking of a number between 1-100")
  print("See if you can guess it within 7 guesses \
    or less")
  print("I will let you know if the number is \
    higher or lower than your guess.")
  print("Here we go!")
```

We will need several variables in our program. We need one to keep track of the number of guesses used. We need one for the player's guess. Finally, we need one to hold our secret number. We will also need to import the random library for this.

```
import random
numGuesses = 0
guess = 0
secretNum = random.randint(1—100)
```

Now we need to prompt players for their guess and then compare it to our secret number. Remember that all input comes in from the keyboard as a string, so we'll need to cast it as an integer. I plan to do this as one of the first steps in the **while** loop.

```
guess = input("What is your first guess: ")
```

Next, we need to set up a way for players to keep guessing until they run out of guesses or guess the number. This sounds like there is repetition, so a **while** loop will work for our solution. Since our **numGuesses** variable starts at 0, our loop's condition needs to have it run while the number of guesses is less than 7. We could also initialize **numGuesses** to 1 and then set our loop condition to be while **numGuesses** <= 7 or equivalently, **numGuesses** < 8. Make sure you understand how all of these are correct ways to set up our condition.

```
while (numGuesses < 7):
```

Then, we have to compare the user's guess to our secret number and provide feedback. Remember, if the secret number is higher than the guess, we provide that information back to the user. Similarly, if the secret number is lower than the guess, we share that information too. We should also let them know how many guesses they have left. And of course, we do let them know if they correctly guessed the number in 7 or fewer guesses.

```
if (guess == secretNum):
  print("You guessed the number in", numGuesses,
     "guesses! The number was", secretNum)
elif (guess < secretNum):
  print("The number is higher than your guess.")
  print("You have", (7 - numGuesses), "guesses \
  left.")
else:
  print("The number is lower than your guess.")
  print("You have", (7 - numGuesses), "guesses \
  left.")
```

If they have not guessed the number, we need to prompt the users for another guess. This line of code should be in the **while** loop so it is indented one level. Since we cast this as an integer as one of the first steps in our **while** loop, and we are not using it as part of the **while** loop's condition, we can use that cast for both *input* statements.

```
guess = input("What is your next guess: ")
```

Once our **while** loop ends, we need to know if it ended because the user guessed the number or because they ran out of guesses. There are several ways to do this. If they guess the correct number, we could set the **numGuesses** variable to be 7 so the loop will stop. The problem with this is that we would not know if they had won the game by guessing the number. We can't distinguish different meanings of **numGuesses** by doing this, so this option is not the best for our case.

Another possibility is to break out of the loop if the user guesses the number correctly. We could set up a condition to see if **numGuesses** less than 7. If it is, then we can assume that the player guessed the number within the allowed number of guesses.

A third option is to use a flag variable and set it to a value when the user correctly guesses the number. This is the option I plan to use. While any of these will work, I think this one is the clearest for someone picking up the program and understanding what it is doing. I will use a variable *win* and set it to *True* when the correct number is guessed. I will define it at the top of the program and initially set it to be False and change it to be true in the `if (guess == secretNum)` block of code.

```
win = True
```

I will also add a check for `win == True` in the `while` loop's condition so I don't keep trying to get users to guess more numbers after they correctly guessed the secret number.

```
while (numGuesses < 7 and win == False):
```

Then, after we are out of the `while` loop, I can set up an *if* statement to determine our final output to users based on whether they guessed the number or not.

There is one very important aspect we have not yet discussed. What happens if the player enters the word "ten" rather than the integer 10? Yep. Our program will crash with an error about not being able to compare a *str* and *int*. We need a way to capture this user error and protect the program from crashing. Fortunately, we have the perfect solution, our `try` and `except` structure. We need to wrap the `try` around our conversion of the user's guess from a string to an integer. If it is successful, we can also add one to the `numGuesses` variable here.

If our attempt to cast the user's guess to an integer fails, then we need to place an error message in the `except` block. Also, our program will continue with the comparisons in the *if/elif* statements after our try:/except structure finishes, whether we have an error or not. We could set a flag if there is an error and add a check for the error flag to be true. Another option is to use our *continue* statement. It will keep us in the `while` loop, but skip everything after the *continue* and go back to the top of our `while` loop to check the condition to see if we continue with another iteration. This is just what we need!

```
try:
  guess = int(guess)
  numGuesses + = 1
except:
  print("Invalid guess. Please enter an \
  integer.")
  continue
```

Now, we should have all the pieces for our Guessing Game to run. Here is one solution for the game.

```
# Name
# Date
# Guessing game using a binary search algorithm

import random

def instructions():
  print("Welcome to the Guessing Game!")
  print("I am thinking of a number between 1—100")
  print("See if you can guess it within 7 guesses \
  or less")
  print("Here we go!")

numGuesses = 0
guess = 0
win = False

# Set secret number
secretNum = random.randint(1,100)

# Call function to display the game instructions
instructions()
```

```
while (numGuesses < 7 and win == False):

  guess = input("\nWhat number do you guess? ")
  try:
    guess = int(guess)
    numGuesses + = 1
  except:
    print("Invalid guess. Please enter an \
    integer.")
    continue

  # Comparisons of secret number to user guess
  if (guess == secretNum):
    print("\nYou guessed the number in",
    numGuesses, "guesses! The number was",
    secretNum)
    win = True
  elif (guess < secretNum):
    print("\nThe number is higher than your \
    guess.")
    print("You have", (7 - numGuesses),
    "guesses left.")
  else:
    print("\nThe number is lower than your \
    guess.")
    print("You have", (7 - numGuesses),
    "guesses left.")

# Print message that they are out of guesses.
if (win == False):
  print("\nYou lost! The number was: ",
  secretNum)
```

Project 4: Guessing Game Reboot!

See if you can code the Guessing Game from the opposite perspective. Rather than the computer thinking of a number and the player guessing it, ask the user to think of a number and provide feedback to the computer to try and guess the number. For my version of the game, I'm going to increase the challenge. Instead of guessing a number between 1 and 100, this version will have the computer guess a number between 1 and 1,000 and we'll get 10 guesses to do it!

The first step is to rewrite the instructions. We need to update the number range from 100 to 1,000 and tell the player that they have to give the higher or lower feedback. Here are my updated instructions, and I am keeping them in a function named instructions() to call when needed. Remember the \ character is used when a single coding statement spans multiple lines. If your code fits on one line, you do not need to use it.

```python
def instructions():
    print("Welcome to the Guessing Game Reboot!")
    print("You think of a number between 1-1,000!")
    print("I will try and guess it in 10 guesses or \
    less.")
    print("\nYes, you read that right! 10 guesses \
    to find 1 number in 1,000 numbers!")
    print("The only requirement is that you tell \
    me if the number is higher or lower than my \
    guess.")
    print("\nLet's find out if this is even \
    possible!")
```

We need to update our variables. We'll still need **numGuesses** and **win**. We'll also need to have our range of numbers so we can calculate our guess based on the midpoint of the range. I called mine *low* and *high* and initialized low to 1 and high to 1,000.

I added a **print()** statement for the user to think of a number. I then kept the same loop setup but updated **numGuesses** to be less than 10 for this program.

```
print("\nThink of a number between 1 and 1,000")
while (numGuesses < 10 and win == False):
```

Next, I added the code for the computer's guess. Each time, it will be the midpoint of our current range, so I add the variables *low* and *high* and then divide by 2, and print the guess. Notice that I also cast the guess to be an integer with the **int()** function since it does not make sense to guess a number with a decimal. I also update the number of guesses I've had so far.

```
compGuess = int((low + high) / 2)
print ("\tMy guess is:", compGuess)
numGuesses + = 1
```

I then ask the user for feedback to find out if I guessed correctly, or if the actual number is higher or lower than my guess. Based on their response, I need to update the range. If the actual number is higher, then my new low range is (my guess + 1). I add 1 to my last guess so I don't include a number I've already guessed and know is wrong in the pool of numbers. Similarly, if my guess was too high and the actual number is lower, I need to update the high end of the range. It is now my guess − 1. I need to subtract one so I don't include my old guess in the new range. I also added a print statement to include how many guesses I have left.

```
if (highLow == 'c'):
  print("\nI guessed the number in", numGuesses,
  "guesses!")
  win = True
elif (highLow == 'h'):
  low = compGuess + 1
  print("\n\tGuesses left:", (10 − numGuesses))
else:
  high = compGuess −1
  print("\n\tGuesses left:", (10 - numGuesses))
```

This repeats until I guess the number or run out of guesses. Here is my completed code. Yours will be similar in structure and messages, but calculating the low and high ranges should be the same, just with different variable names.

```
# Name
# Date
# Guessing game using a binary search algorithm

import random

def instructions():
  print("Welcome to the Guessing Game Reboot!")
  print("You think of a number between 1—1,000!")
  print("I will try and guess it in 10 guesses or \
  less.")
  print("\nYes, you read that right! 10 guesses \
  to find 1 number in 1,000 numbers!")
  print("The only requirement is that you tell \
  me if the number is higher or lower than my \
  guess.")
  print("\nLet's find out if this is even \
  possible!")

numGuesses = 0
low = 1
high = 1000
win = False

# Call the function to display the game
# instructions
instructions()
print("\nThink of a number between 1 and 1,000")
```

```python
while (numGuesses < 10 and win == False):
  # Set the computer's guess to be the midpoint
  # of the current low and high numbers
  compGuess = int((low + high) / 2)
  print ("\tMy guess is:", compGuess)
  numGuesses + = 1
  print("Did I guess it correctly or is the \
  number higher or lower than my guess?")
  highLow = input("Enter 'c' for correct, 'h' for \
  higher, or 'l'for lower")

  # invalid response
  if (highLow ! = "c" and highLow ! = "h" and
  highLow ! = "l"):
    print ("Invalid response. Please enter 'c',
   'h', or 'l'.")
    continue

  # Adjust low and high variables based on user
  response of 'h' or 'l'
  if (highLow == 'c'):
    print("\nI guessed the number in", numGuesses,
    "guesses!")
    win = True
  elif (highLow == 'h'):
    low = compGuess + 1
    print("\n\tGuesses left:", (10 - numGuesses))

  else:
    high = compGuess - 1
    print("\n\tGuesses left:", (10 - numGuesses))
```

```
# Print message that they are out of guesses.
if (win == False):
  print("\nI'm out of guesses. I lost!")
```

Try out your code with a friend or family member!

Project 5: The Challenge Game

Who doesn't like a challenge? I already think you like challenges, otherwise, you would not be reading this book and learning to program! Let's create a game that has challenges for the player to complete when interacting with other characters. We will build a basic structure, but this is a game you can continue to add features to, to make it more challenging and fun, especially for repeat players.

Let's design the basics for our game. The player will meet different characters during their time in the game. Each one will have different tools and skills. Players will experience different outcomes depending on the input they provide to question prompts. The outcome of events will be determined randomly, which adds an element of suspense and surprise to our game. The players will have lives, and once they are out of lives, the game is over. Also, the player who survives enough interactions then wins!

We will have to have instructions so our players will know how to play our game and what they are expected to do. Write these so they set the scene and entice players to want to play your game. In the program, I plan to put these in a function and call it at the start of each new game. This way, our code will be more readable. Here's the start of my instructions in a function named **howToPlay()**. I want to make the instructions feel suspenseful, so I will add **time.sleep()** to add a little bit of a delay. To include this module, I need to import the *time* library.

```
import time
```

```
def howToPlay():
  print("Hello, and welcome to the mysterious \
    forest!")
```

The player will start out with 3 lives. This will go up or down based on decisions made and chance encounters. I defined a variable named *lives* and assigned it an initial value of 3.

```
lives = 3
```

Since the number of lives will determine when the game ends, we should use it in the condition for a **while** loop.

```
while (lives > 0):
```

Before we get too far, we'd better think about the design for the challenges. Our player can interact with several characters, so I will create a list of these characters. Then the character can be chosen at random from the list when they will interact.

```
character = ["healer", "equestrian", "archer",
            "scout", "troll", "goblin"]
```

Each character will have objects that can help or hurt our player. These will also be set up in lists. For example, the healer will have the following objects:

```
healer = ["herbs", "spices", "crystals",
          "potion", "food", "water"]
```

You can keep adding on to the lists. So that you don't have to remember to update the ending number for the random number generator to include all possibilities, use the **len()** command to determine the current length of the list and subtract 1 for the last index position. The index position for a list starts at 0 and goes to the length of the list minus 1. For example, this determines a random number between 0 and length − 1 of the healer objects. Even if I add or remove elements from the list, I won't have to update this code because it will always calculate the current length of the list and subtract 1 to get a valid index position.

```
healer[random.randint(0,(len(healer) -1))]
```

The next part of the program needs to add the interactions with each character. Since we could interact with each one multiple times, we should create a function for each character. If you keep working on this program and add more options to it, you may want to have a separate function for each one. For now, I am going to put them all into one function and pass it the list of characters and a random number to determine which one will be selected each time.

```
def act(actor, position):
```

Then, an *if/elif* statement will be used to determine further actions based on which character is chosen. Here is part of the *if* statement for two of the characters. Notice in the *equestrian* section that I used modulus math to determine if you would be considered a friend or foe.

```
if (actor[position] == "healer"):
   provide = healer[random.randint(0,5)]
   print("The healer welcomes you and will provide \
   you with", provide)
elif (actor[position] == "equestrian"):
   provide = equestrian[random.randint(0,3)]

   if (position% 2 == 0):
      print("The equestrian welcomes you and will \
      provide you with", provide)
```

```
    else:
        print("You startled the equestrian. He raises \
        his", provide, "and charges at you!")
```

You would complete an *if/elif* condition for each character in your game.

In addition to the lives, we should add a counter, so if we live through enough encounters with characters, we make it through the mysterious forest alive! I'm going to call my variable *events*. If the player makes it through 7 events, then they have made it through the forest and get a congratulatory message! I need to add one to the *events* variable during each pass of the `while` loop. It differs from lives since lives can go up or down by 1 or 2, plus lives can stay the same based on the character and action involved. Here is the code to print an appropriate message based on the value of *events* at the end of the program.

```
if (events == 7 and lives > 0):
    print("\nYou survived where many others failed \
        in their attempt! You are clever and lucky!")
else:
    print("\nYou failed in your quest to cross the \
        mystical forest. Better luck next time!")
```

One way to make our game more interesting would be to add an opportunity for the player to accept or reject items from the healer and scout and fight or run when under attack by the others. In this example, I added a prompt under the healer's option for the user to take what is being offered. I set up another list of possible results and pick one at random.

```
react = input("\nDo you take it from the healer: \
    'y' or 'n'")
print(healerAct[random.randint(0, len(healerAct)
    -1)])
```

Here is our code so far. You can see there are many opportunities to continue making it more complex and involving the player more in the possible outcomes. This makes it more fun to play!

```python
# Name
# Date
# Game to find your way through a forest with
# challenges along the way.

import time, random

def howToPlay():
  print("Hello, and welcome to the mysterious \
  forest!")
  print("You will have to use your wits, along \
  with a little luck, to make it out of this \
  mysterious, but magical forest.")
  time.sleep(2)
  print("Many who enter are never heard from \
  again...")
  print("You will make decisions throughout that \
  will determine your fate.")
  time.sleep(2)
  print("\nGood luck!")
  time.sleep(2)

def act(actor, position):
  if (actor[position] == "healer"):
    provide = healer[random.randint(0,(len(healer)
    - 1))]
```

```
      print("\nThe healer welcomes you and will \
      provide you with", provide + ".")
      liveOrDie = 1
      time.sleep(2)
      react = input("\nDo you take it from the \
      healer: 'y' or 'n'? ")

      print(healerAct[random.randint(0, len
      (healerAct) - 1)])

elif (actor[position] == "equestrian"):
   provide = equestrian[random.
   randint(0,(len(equestrian) - 1))]

   if (position% 2 == 0):
      print("\nThe equestrian welcomes you and will \
      provide you with", provide)
      liveOrDie = 1
      time.sleep(2)
      react = input("\nDo you accept this from the \
      equestrian: 'y' or 'n'")
   else:
      print("\nYou startled the equestrian. He \
      raises his", provide, "and charges at you!")
      liveOrDie = - 1

   print(equestrianAct[random.randint(0,
   len(equestrianAct) - 1)])

elif (actor[position] == "archer"):
   provide = archer[random.randint(0,(len(archer)
   - 1))]
```

```
  if (position% 3 == 0):
    print("\nThe archer offers to accompany you \
    to the edge of the river.")
    liveOrDie = 1

    time.sleep(2)
    react = input("\nDo you graciously accept \
    or remain fiercely independent: 'accept' or \
    'alone'? ")
  else:
    print("\nThe archer raises her", provide,
    "and warns you to leave now!")
    liveOrDie = 0
    time.sleep(2)

    react = input("\nWhat will it be: 'fight' or \
    'run'? ")

    print(archerAct[random.randint(0,
    len(archerAct) -1)])

elif (actor[position] == "scout"):
  provide = scout[random.randint(0,(len(scout)
  -1))]
  print("\nThe scout offers you a", provide, "to \
  help provide you safe passage.")
  liveOrDie = 1

  print(scoutAct[random.randint(0, len(scoutAct)
  -1)])

elif (actor[position] == "monster"):
  provide = monster[random.randint(0,
  (len(monster) -1))]
```

```python
    print("\nThe monster comes at you and attempts \
    to maim you with his", provide + "!")
    liveOrDie = -2

    print(monsterAct[random.randint(0,
    len(monsterAct) - 1)])

    return liveOrDie

# declare and initialize variables and lists
lives = 3
events = 0
character = ["healer", "equestrian", "archer",
    "scout", "monster"]
healer = ["herbs", "spices", "crystals",
    "potion", "food", "water"]
healerAct = ["\n\tYou have angered the healer! \
    RUN",
    "\n\tThe healer will accompany you to the \
    valley.",
    "\n\tThe healer wants you to stay forever and \
    learn to be a healer too."]

# add acts for rest of characters
equestrian = ["shield", "bayonet", "sword",
    "battle axe"]
equestrianAct = ["\n\tThe equestrian recognizes \
    you and scoops you up onto his horse!",
    "\n\tYou turn to run and see a huge monster \
    behind you that the equestrian skewers saving \
    your life!",
    "\n\tYou grab his weapon and knock him off his \
    horse. You then jump on and ride away!"]
```

```
archer = ["shield", "bow and arrow", "spear",
  "blowgun"]
archerAct = ["\n\tYour shirt has been speared,
  trapping you onto a tree! How embarrassing!",
  "\n\tYou bow and make a sign of deference. The \
  archer leads you back to camp.",
  "\n\tYou run away in a zigzag pattern hoping \
  not to be hit by arrows!"]

scout = ["whistle", "compass", "map", "costume"]
scoutAct = ["\n\tYou accept the item and head off \
  through the woods",
  "\n\tYou ask the scout to show you his ways to \
  help you survive your journey.",
  "\n\tYou make too much noise and awaken the \
  monsters!"]

monster = ["bad breath", "rocks", "club",
  "claws"]
monsterAct = ["\n\tThe monster knocks you to the \
  ground and grabs you in his hairy paw!",
  "\n\tYou tickle the monster and he falls to the \
  ground laughing allowing you to escape!",
  "\n\tYou pull a splinter from the monster's toe \
  whereby he owes you his undying allegiance and \
  safe passage forever!"]

# main program

# call instructions
howToPlay()
```

```
while (lives > 0 and events < 7):
    events = events + 1
    # call the character to interact with
    health = act(character,
    random.randint(0,(len(character) -1)))

    # calculate impact of health on lives
    lives = lives + health

    time.sleep(2)

    if (events == 7 and lives > 0):
        print("\nYou survived where many others failed \
        in their attempt! You are clever and lucky!")
    else:
        print("\nYou failed in your quest to cross the \
        mystical forest. Better luck next time!")
```

You can continue adding new characters and new objects, tools, potions, and weapons to existing characters along with possibilities for actions. You can also prompt the player for more interaction. This game can get more creative and intricate as you continue working on it. Your friends will enjoy it and make suggestions or requests as well. Enjoy the creation and the coding!

As you think of what to create with your next program, you are only limited by your imagination! You have the basic tools of Python, which provide a lot of possibilities. You can always check the official Python 3 documentation to find other features you may need. Explore and have fun!

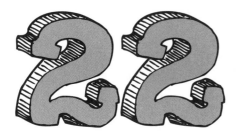

Micro:bit

The BBC micro:bit, created in the UK, is a **microcontroller**, meaning a very small computer. It is very popular with programmers, hobbyists, and tinkerers young and old alike! It has made its way into education as well and helps students of all ages quickly program, enabling them to see new possibilities and understand concepts. It is inexpensive, easy to use and program, and we can do many, many things with it! Therefore, we are going to continue learning to program by using a micro:bit with microPython which is a subset of Python.

The micro:bit is smaller than a typical playing card, and comes with:

- 25 LED lights.

- 2 programmable buttons.

- A reset button.

- An accelerometer to detect motion.

- A compass to determine direction.

- A Bluetooth antenna.

- A USB connector.

- A battery connection point.

Getting Started

To get started, we need a micro:bit and a micro USB cable. The cable may come with the micro:bit when you purchase one, but any micro USB cable will work. As of the publishing date of this book, the cost of a micro:bit was $17.50, making it very affordable! You can program without a micro:bit. However, to test and run your code, you will need a micro:bit. There are some emulators available on the web for use with block coding rather than microPython. Hopefully, there will be an emulator for microPython use soon!

Remember that the margins in this book are smaller than the micro:bit IDE where you'll be writing your code. As a result, examples here sometimes spread code over multiple lines. You should keep a line of code on one line in your program to avoid potential syntax errors. You'll also notice here that I sometimes use parentheses around the condition for if and while statements and sometimes, I do not. This is to demonstrate for you that Python and MicroPython do not need the parentheses, and you do not receive an error if you do use them. Remember that other programming languages require the parentheses, so it's a good habit to develop. It will also make learning a new programming language a little bit easier.

When you open the micro:bit box, a safety guide is included with the same information in multiple languages. This is the paper you probably immediately set aside. Pick it back up and read it so you do not inadvertently damage your micro:bit. Several key points in the safety warnings:

- Keep the micro:bit in the antistatic bag when you're not using it.
- Handle the micro:bit by the edges.
- Be sure your hands are dry when handling the micro:bit.
- Keep metal objects off the micro:bit especially when in use or you could short it out.
- Do not store the micro:bit in a too hot or a too cold environment.

There are other safety measures, so please be familiar with them!

- Each of the LED lights is programmable, so words and designs can be displayed.
- Connect the micro:bit to your computer with the micro USB cable.
- The LED light will begin to flash a message to you to get started. It will take you through several steps to help you get familiar with it.

The first task has an arrow pointing to the left button, labeled "button A." Press it.

↓

Then press the button B on the right.

↓

Shake the micro:bit to see the LED lights make a design!

↓

Chase a dot that moves around the screen by tilting the micro:bit.

- After you have done all these activities with the micro:bit, using your computer, navigate to your file directory to see the drive the micro:bit is using. Click on the micro:bit drive to see the files.

- Double click on the MICROBIT.HTML file to open the micro:bit website.

Programming the Micro:bit

We can write our code for the micro:bit using either an online IDE (Integrated Development Environment) or download one. If you do not have reliable wireless Internet access, then download and install the mu-editor. You may prefer to use this anyway, as it is easy to use. It is an IDE, available for Windows, Mac OS, Linux, and Raspberry Pi. Use your web browser and search engine to find a site for :mu download.

The micro:bit can be programmed in several ways. We are going to use Python. The micro:bit Python editor includes quite a few images and precoded modules for us to use. MicroPython is a subset of the same Python programming language the first part of this book uses, but it is designed to work with microcontrollers like the micro:bit by optimizing the functions and methods we can use.

From the microbit.org/code website, scroll down to find the Python Editor and click the Let's Code button. This site has a link to the Python editor from multiple locations, so you will find it no matter which page of the site you are on. You can also go there directly using the link: https://python.microbit.org/v/1.1.

The micro:bit online Python editor will open. A sample program is already preloaded. I hope you are not surprised that it is the **"Hello, World!"** program! You may recall that many programming languages use it to be able to quickly make sure everything is working properly.

```python
# Add Your Python Code here. E.g.
from microbit import*

while True:
    display.scroll('Hello, World!')
    display.show(Image.HEART)
    sleep(2000)
```

- To save the file to your computer, click the save button, second from the top left.

  Be sure you know where downloaded files go on your computer. You may have the option to change the program name and file location. I created a folder for all of my micro:bit programs and downloaded this program to that location. I highly recommend you create a folder and call it *microbit programs* or something similar so you can find or search for your programs later.

- Click the download button on the top far left. This will download a file with the *.hex* file extension.

  Once it successfully downloads, it will need to be "flashed" or loaded into the micro:bit's memory. To do this, drag and drop the .hex file to the micro:bit drive location on your computer. Your micro:bit will flash for a few moments while it is loading. You may also see a progress bar on your screen. When finished, the micro:bit will run your program.

After seeing the message, **"Hello, world!"** flash across the screen, let's change the code to replace **"world"** with your name. Switch back to the micro:bit coding location. Using the code below as a guide, change line 6 where it says **'Hello, your Name!'** to use your actual name.

```
# Hello yourName program
from mocrobit import*

while True:
    display.scroll('Hello, yourName!')
    display.show(Image.HEART)
    sleep(2000)
```

You can download the program without saving it to your computer first, so let's do that this time. Be sure to save it to your computer once you have it tested and working the way you want it to function. Otherwise, it will be gone, and you will have to recreate it. Then drag the .hex file to the micro:bit location where it is connected to your device. It will flash for a moment again, then you should see your name in lights! (At least micro:bit lights.)

If you do not see **"Hello, your name!"**, then there is an error with your code. The micro:bit will scroll a message about the error and provide a line number. It may say syntax error, but not be able to provide much more information than that. The message can be hard to read, but it will repeat if you miss part of it. Follow the suggested steps from Chapter 7 on testing and debugging to find and correct the error. Then save the new version, download it, and drag the .hex file to the micro:bit drive. Hopefully it will work this time, but if not, repeat the troubleshooting steps to debug your code.

A Closer Look

Let's start by looking more closely at the micro:bit code we just used. Here is the code:

```
1 # Hello yourName program
2 from microbit import *
3
4 while True:
5   display.scroll('Hello, yourName!')
6   display.show(Image.HEART)
7 sleep(2000)
```

- Line 1 is a comment with the purpose of our program. Remember comments are ignored by the computer and are for our benefit.

- Line 2 is the `import` statement. We use that to pull in prewritten Python code to our program. This line pulls in everything from the micro:bit library.

- Line 3 is a blank line to separate sections of code for readability. Blank lines are ignored by the computer.

- Line 4 is a repetitive statement, the `while` loop. Notice that it is a deliberate infinite loop in the format, `while True:` Remember a `while` loop will run as long as a condition is true, and this condition is explicitly set up using the Python reserved Boolean value, `True`.

- Line 5 will scroll through the letters in `"Hello, your Name!"` using the micro:bit's LED light grid. Notice the use of the command `display`. We used the `print()` built-in function earlier. `display` works with turning on the LED lights in the micro:bit's 5 by 5 grid rather than printing to a screen. We used the `.scroll()` program from the `display` module in this program statement.

- Line 6 shows a premade heart shape image using the LED lights and the `display` command. This time, we used the `.show()` program from the *display* module.

- Line 7 pauses the program for 2 seconds so we can see the heart shape for that long. Otherwise, as soon as it displayed the heart, it would move on to the next command or end the program, and we'd barely have a chance to see it!

Since the while loop is still true, the program will repeat the scrolling display of `"Hello, World!"` and then the HEART image. You can stop it by disconnecting the USB cable from your computer.

Micro:bit Images

As mentioned earlier, the micro:bit has a 5 by 5 grid of LED lights. There are quite a few images provided with the micro:bit to display on it. Let's try a few out.

Here is the current list of images that are available with the micro:bit.

Animals	Emotions	Objects	Shapes
Image.BUTTERFLY	Image.ANGRY	Image.CHESSBOARD	Image.DIAMOND
Image.COW	Image.ASLEEP (bored)	Image.GHOST	Image.DIAMOND_SMALL
Image.DUCK	Image.CONFUSED	Image.HOUSE	Image.HEART
Image.GIRAFFE	Image.FABULOUS	Image.PACMAN	Image.HEART_SMALL
Image.RABBIT	Image.HAPPY	Image.PITCHFORK	Image.MEH
Image.SNAKE	Image.SAD	Image.ROLLERSKATE	Image.MUSIC_CROTCHET
Image.TORTOISE	Image.SILLY	Image.SKULL	Image.MUSIC_QUAVER
	Image.SMILE	Image.STICKFIGURE	Image.MUSIC_QUAVERS
	Image.SURPRISED	Image.SWORD	Image.NO
		Image.TARGET	Image.SQUARE
		Image.TSHIRT	Image.SQUARE_SMALL
		Image.TRIANGLE	Image.XMAS
		Image.TRIANGLE_LEFT	Image.YES
		Image.UMBRELLA	

Let's modify the code from our **"Hello, World!"** and heart program. Delete Line 3 which is the **display.scroll("Hello, World!")** statement. Change Line 4 to display an image of your choice. All you have to change is the word HEART since the rest of it stays the same.

```
1 from microbit import *
2 while True:
3   display.scroll('Hello, World!')
4   display.show(Image.HEART)
5   sleep(2000)
```

If I wanted to see the rabbit for two seconds, I would change Line 4 to show:

```
4 display.show(Image.RABBIT)
```

Remember to download the modified code to your computer, and then drag the .hex file to the micro:bit drive location.

Try a few of these out to see what they look like on your micro:bit.

Making Your Own Images

While there are quite a few premade images, there will be times when an image we want to display does not exist. The good news is we can make our own images!

The LEDs on the micro:bit are in a grid of 5 rows by 5 columns. Each LED can be assigned a value between 0–9, where 0 is off and 9 is as bright as the LED can display. We have to set up the grid a line at a time when designing our image. Notice the colon: at the end of each row.

`00000:`	Each LED is off.
`02468:`	Each LED is brighter than the one beside it.
`00500:`	Only one column is on at half brightness.
`03530:`	A pattern
`98765:`	Finish the row.

We need to store our grid in a variable, and I'll use the variable name `pic1` since this image is only to show how to set one up. It's not a picture of anything, otherwise, I would a more descriptive variable name.

We also need to use the reserved word *Image* and put our grid in parentheses and double quotation marks.

```
pic1 = Image("00000:"
             "02468:"
             "00500:"
             "03530:"
             "98765:")
```

This image is now defined to our program, and we can refer to it as `pic1` when we want to use it. The grid only has to be set up once for each image in our program. To display the image we created, the format is slightly different. Since it is not a known image in the micro:bit library, we just have to put the variable name that is storing our grid layout in the parentheses after the *show* function.

```
display.show(pic1)
```

You can also define an image in one line. Writing the grid rows vertically helps ensure you don't skip a row or column, but both are equally correct.

```
pic2 = Image("00900:05550:77777:05550:11111: ")
```

Notice in this format that the double quotation marks are only at the beginning and end of the entire grid pattern, and the colon still separates each row of the grid.

Animating Images

Here's a bonus! We can use our still images, either built-in ones, those we create, or a combination of both, to create an animation. Animation is simply still images showing one after the other quickly. Our eyes perceive movement!

We will use a *list* of still images to create this illusion of movement. Refer to chapter 16 to review lists if necessary. Remember that lists can store more than one value at a time. The different values are separated by commas, and square brackets are used around all the values.

```
list = [image1, image2, image3, image4]
```

The `display.show()` function will show each image in our list, one after the other. We need to add extra information to the `display.show()` function so it will know how long to pause between displaying each image in our list. The delay variable handles this. We need to give it a time in milliseconds: 1000 milliseconds = 1 second.

```
display.show(list, delay = 300)
```

The above `display.show` statement will only execute once. If we want it to keep repeating the implied movement, we can add the `loop = True` option in our `display.show()` statement.

```
display.show(list, loop = True, delay = 300)
```

If you ever want to clear the micro:bit screen, use this command:

```
display.clear()
```

Let's create a list of images and set up a `display` statement to make them look like they are moving. The micro:bit library has images that we can use in a list to test our animation code. The micro:bit library provides a series of twelve images for a clock face, one for each hour, that you can put in a list and display. Also, there are arrows pointing in different directions that work well to animate. Try it with other images and some of your own. Have fun!

```
clocks = [Image.CLOCK1, Image.CLOCK2, Image.
CLOCK3, Image.CLOCK4, Image.CLOCK5, Image.CLOCK6,
Image.CLOCK7, Image.CLOCK8, Image.CLOCK9, Image.
CLOCK10, Image.CLOCK11, Image.CLOCK12]
display.show(clocks, loop = True, delay = 350)
arrows = [Image.ARROW_N, Image.ARROW_NE, Image.
ARROW_E, Image.ARROW_SE, Image.ARROW_S, Image.
ARROW_SW, Image.ARROW_W, Image.ARROW_NW]
display.show(arrows, loop = True, delay = 300)
```

Buttons on the Micro:bit

The micro:bit has two buttons on the front of it. The buttons are labeled "A" on the left side and "B" on the right side.

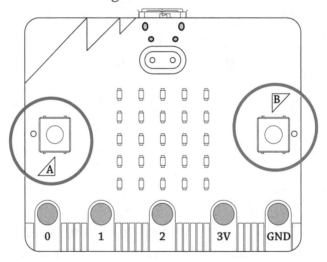

The microPython code provides a way to find out how many times a button has been pressed using:

```
button_a
button_b
```

As you probably guessed, `button_a` stores the number of times it has been pressed, and `button_b` stores the number of times it was pressed. The number will always be in integer. (There are no half presses needing a float!)

Now, we need a way to share the number stored in `button_a` or `button_b`. MicroPython provides a block of code, `get_presses`, which is a *method*. Methods are blocks of code that do an action. In this case, it gives us a way to get the number of button presses. The format is:

```
Object + . + methodName
button_a.get_presses()
button_b.get_presses()
```

Notice the method name has parentheses after the name, just as our functions do.

As usual, we need to store the number of presses in a variable. We can name the variable what we want, but remember there are rules such as not using a reserved word, and we do want it to be descriptive. See Chapter 8 on variables to review the naming rules and conventions.

```
numAPresses = button_a.get_presses()
```

Once we have stored the number in a variable, we can work with the variable without having to keep asking the method to go find out how many presses there were. We only need to use `get_presses()` again when the number of presses has changed.

There is also a Boolean method that comes in handy with buttons. The `is_pressed()` method will return true if a button was pressed or false if it was not. Remember that when we set up conditions for `if` statements or `while` loops, they evaluate to be true or false.

The next question is what can we do with the number of button presses and when? We will use **Event-Driven Programming**. This is where we use an event that occurs to trigger a section of code to execute. A smartphone uses event-driven programming. It is in ready mode waiting for a swipe, tap, text message, audio, or other event to trigger different apps to run its code.

We have already seen how to set up an infinite `while` loop. This will put our micro:bit into wait mode. Then we can set up a selection statement using a condition to test if either button is pressed as an event and do something when it is. Refer back to Chapter 14 on selection statements to refresh your memory if needed.

```python
1 # We always need this import statement.
2 from microbit import *
# Set up an infinite loop to wait for an event.
3 while True:
4   if (button_a.is_pressed()):
5       display.show(Image.STICKFIGURE)
6   elif (button_b.is_pressed()):
7       display.scroll("Here I am!")
8       # This will clear the micro:bit's screen
9       display.clear()
```

In the code below, we used a compound condition using `and`. microPython can handle compound conditions that we can create using the logical operators `and`, `or`, and `not`. In our code, if both buttons are pushed at the same time, then a ghost image is displayed. See Chapter 15 on logical operators if you need to review.

```python
1 from microbit import *
2 # Set up an infinite loop to wait for an
  # event.
3 while True:
4   if (button_a.is_pressed() and button_b.
    is_pressed()):
```

```
5      display.show(Image.GHOST)
6      # This will clear the micro:bit's screen.
7      display.clear()
```

There is another button on the opposite side of the micro:bit from **button_a** and **button_b**. It is the **reset** button. If you press it, either accidentally or on purpose while a program is running, the program will refresh and start over from the beginning.

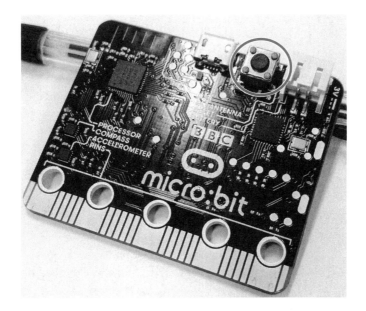

Source: Ravi Kotecha

Micro:bit Pins

Along the bottom of the micro:bit is a metal strip with holes and line separators. These are called the I/O pins (meaning Input/Output) and there are 25 of them. The sections with holes are labeled 0, 1, 2, 3V, and GND. Remember that Python, along with many other programming languages, starts numbering at 0. Each pin has a number associated with it, even though the numbers for the smaller pins are not marked on the micro:bit. We can reference each one in a program using the **pinN** object where N is the number of the pin: **pin1.**

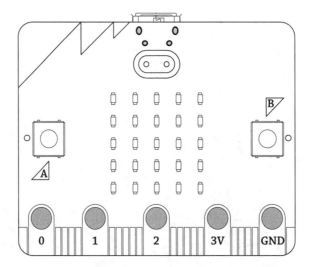

- Pins 0, 1, and 2 are referred to as "general purpose input and output," which is often shown as GPIO. They are also able to convert analog to digital power, and this is abbreviated as ADC, which is how it is usually written.

- The 3V stands for 3 volts of power. This means it can be used to connect to peripherals, such as speakers.

- GND stands for ground. If you are working on a carpeted surface, briefly touch something metal to discharge any static buildup to avoid short-circuiting your micro:bit. *Never* connect the 3V and GND connectors, or your micro:bit will be damaged.

Since the human body produces a current, we can be a connector to test our pins. To test **pin0**, since it is easiest to reach, let's set up the following code:

```
1 from microbit import *
2
3   while True:
4     if pin0.is_touched():
5           display.show(Image.YES)
6     else:
7           display.show(Image.NO)
```

To test the code, be sure you are touching the GND pin with one hand and the 0 pin with the other. The check mark should display when you are touching it and the X mark when the connection is interrupted.

There are 20 of the small pins, each with a different function. Many of these pins share functionality with one of the LEDs or buttons. If you are using it for a different purpose, then you cannot also use the LED or button it is shared with at the same time. It is recommended by micro:bit that an edge connector be used to access these, and it does make it a lot easier. This does not come with the basic micro:bit, but can be purchased separately.

- **pin3** shared with LED Column 1

- **pin4** shared with LED Column 2

- **pin5** shared with Button A

- **pin6** shared with LED Column 9

- **pin7** shared with LED Column 8

- **pin10** shared with LED Column 3

- **pin11** shared with Button B

- **pins 17** and **18** wired to the 3V pin

- **pins 21** and **22** wired to the GND pin

After purchasing an extender, refer to the micro:bit documentation or projects for information on how to connect and code the small pins.

There are many devices that can be used with the various pins. The official micro:bit website lists resellers of their devices and accessories. Alligator clips are useful for connecting to the large pins. Select several resellers and visit their sites to find a variety of accessories for purchase: https://microbit.org/resellers/.

Micro:bit's Accelerometer

The micro:bit has a way to measure direction using a built-in accelerometer. The image below shows the three directions the micro:bit can detect movement.

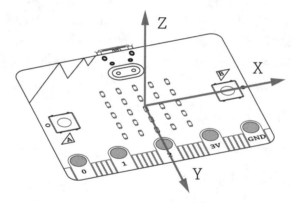

The three axes of the micro:bit accelerometer.
Source: Ugopedia.

- The x axis measures from left to right.

- The y axis measures forward and backward.

- The z axis measures movement up and down.

When an axis is level, the measurement is 0. MicroPython provides methods to access the value of each axis, measured in milli-g's, the standard for this. The methods are:

```
get_x()
get_y()
get_z()
```

We can set up a selection statement to do different actions based on the values that show where each axis is positioned. It's a good idea to use a range for determining if an axis is level. The accelerometer is pretty sensitive, so it will be difficult to get and keep a level measurement if it is not lying flat (and that's no fun!).

```
1 from microbit import
2 # Set up an infinite loop to keep measuring
  # the axes.
3 while (True):
4     directX = accelerometer.get_x()
5     directY = accelerometer.get_y()
6     directZ = accelerometer.get_z()
7
8     if (directX >= 25):
          # Use arrows to show the direction.
9         display.show(Image.ARROW_E)
10    elif (directX <= -25):
11        display.show(Image.ARROW_W)
12    else:
13        display.show("lvl")
```

You can incorporate the *y* and *z* axes too, along with compound conditions to do a variety of actions based on how the micro:bit is positioned.

Micro:bit Gestures

Now we can really have some fun with the micro:bit and its accelerometer. Similar to other devices, the micro:bit can use gestures based on the accelerometer values. The method

```
accelerometer.current_gesture()
```

returns one of the following gestures:

up	face up
down	face down
left	3g # These are g-force (gravity) detections.
right	6g
freefall	8g
shake	

We can use these in a program to do an action based on the gesture detected. We also have two new methods we can incorporate for the accelerometer.

```
accelerometer.current_gesture()
accelerometer.was_gesture()
```

```
1 from microbit import *
2 # Set up an infinite loop to keep measuring
  # the axes.
3 while (True):
4     gesture = accelerometer.current_gesture()
5
```

```
6      if (gesture == "shake"):
7          # Use the arrows to show the direction.
8          display.show(Image.NO)
9      else:
10             display.show(Image.YES)
```

Micro:bit Compass

The micro:bit also comes with a built-in compass. A calibration program is included with the micro:bit import statement because you need to calibrate the compass at the beginning of a program so it will give you accurate values. The command to use is:

```
compass.calibrate()
```

If you don't include the command in your code, the micro:bit will display directions to calibrate. The micro:bit has to be moved around, and calibration is not complete until all the grid lights are on. A smiley face will then be displayed so you know it is finished calibrating. Then your program will run.

The method `compass.heading()` returns an integer that represents the degrees from 1 to 360, (the number of degrees in a circle), that the micro:bit is facing. We can set up the code for the micro:bit to show us the direction it is facing. We will just use `North, South, East,` and `West`. You can modify the code later to add NE, SE, SW, and NW if you want to do so. We can use a nested *if* statement for the degrees because as soon as a condition is met, the rest of the conditions do not need to be checked.

- `North` will be greater than 315 degrees or less than 45 degrees.

- `East` will be between 46 and 135 degrees.

- `South` will be between 136 and 225 degrees.

- `West` will be between 226 and 314 degrees.

Using these, we need to set up our conditions. We set up the degree conditions to go around the circle in clockwise order.

```
1 from microbit import *
2
3 compass.calibrate()
4 while (True):
5    direction = compass.heading()
6    if (direction <= 45 or direction > = 315):
7        display.show("N")
8    elif (direction <= 135):
9        display.show("E")
10   elif (direction <= 225):
11       display.show("S")
12   else:
13       display.show("W")
```

Be aware that the compass and the LED grid are on opposite sides of the micro:bit, so adjust the direction for the way you are holding the micro:bit, if necessary. That's all there is to it!

Random Numbers

Random numbers are used in many computer programs, especially games. Fortunately, microPython provides several random-number-based functions we can use. First, we have to include another **import** statement, specifically for the random library.

```
import random
```

To use the programs in this library, we use the same format we have been using: the folder name.program name. A frequently used one is **randint(start, end). Start** represents the beginning number, and **end** represents the ending boundary for the random integer to be generated. Both of these are included in the possibilities.

```
num = random.randint(1,6)     # Simulates rolling a
                                6-sided die
```

Another frequently used random number program is **randrange (0, N)**. A random integer is generated between 0 and N, where N is an integer. In this case, 0 is included in the list of possibilities, but the ending number is excluded. Therefore, if you want a number between 0 and 100, write it as:

```
number = random.randrange(0,101)   # The second
                                     number goes
                                     up to but is not
                                     included.
```

Random numbers are good for guessing games and selecting paths to explore in games, along with simulating dice rolls. Let's say you and a friend arrive at the vending machine at the same time. You just happen to have a micro:bit and battery in your pocket, so you agree to use the micro:bit to generate a random number to decide who goes first. Let's code it so you'll be ready should this scenario or any other event needing a random number ever occur!

Let's think about our setup with the micro:bit. We have two buttons available to use, but we really only need one of them to start the random number generation. Pick the button you want to use for your program. I plan to use button B. (Maybe I should randomly generate a number to determine which button to use!) When the micro:bit senses that **button_b** has been pressed, then we want it to generate a random number.

We'll use one of the modules from the **random** library. This tells us we'd better not forget to import this library. It goes at the top of our program after the **microbit import** statement.

```
import random
```

We want our program to generate more than one random number at a time, so it sounds like a loop will be needed. We'll use the same structure we have been with a `while (True):` loop.

```
while (True):
```

Inside our `while` loop, we'll need to check when the `button_b.is_pressed()` event occurs. When it does, we'll want to generate a random number. I'm keeping mine in the range 0–9 so it won't scroll, but you easily could have it do so. I'll display the number and we could end the program with this. It works just fine.

However, if two people are using this program on the micro:bit to see who goes first, then it will be difficult to see when the second player's number begins, especially if the same random number is generated and it's a tie. Therefore, I'll clear the screen and wait to generate and display the next random number when `button_b` is pressed again.

```
display.clear()
```

While this works, unfortunately, the number generated flashes on the screen and then disappears. The micro:bit runs the commands so quickly that we don't have time to see or show the number to anyone else. So, let's include a delay with the sleep command so it shows for a second, which is 1,000 milliseconds. The sleep command uses milliseconds. You can increase this to be more time if needed: 1500 is 1.5 seconds and 2000 would be 2 seconds.

```
sleep(1000)
```

This should take care of generating and displaying the number for a reasonable amount of time. Here's our completed code. Remember, to run it, you need to download it to your computer, and then drag the program's *.hex* file to the micro:bit drive. It will install and then wait for the `button_b` event to trigger the code to generate and display the number.

```
# random number generator
from microbit import *
import random

while (True):
  if (button_b.is_pressed()):
    num = random.randint(0,9)
    display.show(num)
    sleep(1000)
    display.clear()
```

If we wanted to have a larger pool of numbers, then update the range for the `random.randint(0, ending range)`. For numbers more than one digit long, I would also change the `display.show()` command to be `display.scroll()`. It makes it easier to read and understand the larger number.

```
# random number generator from 0 — 100
from microbit import *
import random

while (True):
  if (button_b.is_pressed()):
    num = random.randint(0,100)
    display.scroll(num)
    sleep(1000)
    display.clear()
```

Words of Wisdom Game

We can build upon the structure from the random numbers to create an advice game. Depending on the number generated, we can use it to display words of wisdom. How can we set this up? We will need to have a list with possible responses loaded in it. The number generated will be used as the index position for the list to determine which message to display. We will also need to give instructions to the seeker of wisdom or, in other words, our player.

We'll need to keep our micro:bit and random library import statements. Then we need to display some instructions for our player. Instead of having to press a button, let's use the accelerometer this time. We'd better provide instructions since that may not be intuitive to our users.

```
display.scroll("Shake me to play!")
```

Then we need to build a list of phrases to display. You can make these as funny or realistic as you want! I named my list variable **wisdom**, although I'm not sure my phrases are all particularly wise.

```
wisdom = ["Go for it!", "Make lemonade!",
    "Think", "Choose better!", "Be silly!",
    "Have fun!", "Be kind"]
```

We need our usual **while(True):** loop to set our program in motion. Indented under the loop, we'll use the **accelerometer.current_gesture()** method. I set the current motion to be stored in a variable named **gesture**. I then use that in an *if* statement's condition. We could combine that into one combined statement: *if* **(accelerometer.current_gesture() == "shake")**, but either is correct.

If the motion is **"shake"**, then we'll generate a random number to determine which words of wisdom will be displayed. The **randint()** module takes beginning and ending numbers for our range, and both are included. As we add more words of advice to our program, we don't want to have to remember to also update the random number possibilities, so let's use the `len()` method again.

This method returns the length of a list or string, so we can pass it our list, in this case, named `wisdom`. We have to subtract one from the length for our `randit()` ending value. Just as a reminder, the length of a list is the number of elements in it. Our list, `wisdom`, has 7 elements in it, so the length is 7. However, the index position of the first element is 0, the second element is 1, and so on. The last element can be referenced as the length minus one or `len(wisdom) - 1`.

```
num = random.randint(0,len(wisdom) - 1)
```

We could also use a second variable to calculate the length minus one value.

```
end = len(wisdom) — 1
```

We can then use the variable `end` as the stopping point for our range of numbers.

```
num = random.randint(0,end)
```

Both ways of setting this up are correct.

Finally, we display the words of wisdom at the index position that was randomly selected. I included a pause of one second and then clear the display in case someone else wants to immediately shake the micro:bit for their words of advice! Here is the full program.

```
# Words of Wisdom program
from microbit import *
import random
wisdom = ["Go for it!", "Make lemonade!",
```

```
        "Think", "Choose better!", "Be silly!",
        "Have fun!", "Be kind"]
display.scroll("Shake me to play!")

while (True):
    gesture = accelerometer.current_gesture()

    if (gesture == "shake"):
        num = random.randint(0,len(wisdom) - 1)
        display.scroll(wisdom[num])
        sleep(1000)
        display.clear()
```

Temperature Program

Here's a cool feature of the micro:bit. The processor on the chip also measures temperature! A method aptly named `temperature()` is used to capture the current temperature where the micro:bit is located. The value provided will be an integer and represents the temperature in Celsius.

To start our program, we need our usual import of the micro:bit library. This provides us the use of the `temperature()` function. We'll take a temperature reading by calling the function and storing the value in a variable named `tempC`, for temperature in Celsius.

```
tempC = temperature()
```

Since I am used to temperature readings in Fahrenheit, I'm going to convert the temperature from Celsius to Fahrenheit. The formula is (Celsius * 9/5) + 32. One thing to note here is that our Celsius temperature reading is an integer. When we divide by 5, we'll get a decimal value.

We have a design decision to make here. Do we want to cast our value as an integer and truncate the decimal portion or keep it? If we want to keep it, then no changes are needed. However, if we only want an integer, we'll need to use the **int()** function to convert our temperature with the *float* data type to be an *int* datatype. I just need a general idea of the temperature, so I'll convert it to be an integer.

```
tempF = int(((tempC * 9) / 5) + 32)
```

By the way, the temperature reading from the micro:bit is a couple of degrees warmer than the actual temperature due to the heat generated by the processor. You can adjust for this by taking several readings to determine how much it is usually off and then subtracting that amount.

Since I'm interested in becoming more comfortable with temperature in Celsius, I want to include both temperatures. I'll print the temperature in Celsius first, then in Fahrenheit. I'll include a **C** or **F** after the appropriate one to avoid confusion. I also have to cast the integer temperature variables, *tempC* and *tempF*, to be strings with the **str()** function before printing. That's a requirement of the *display* modules.

```
# Read and display the temperature
# Convert from Celsius to Fahrenheit
from microbit import *

tempC = temperature()
display.scroll(str(tempC) + "C")
tempF = int(((tempC * 9) / 5) + 32)
display.scroll(str(tempF) + "F")
sleep(1000)
```

Notice this only takes and displays the temperature reading once. If I look away and miss the number scrolling across the micro:bit, then I'm out of luck. We could wrap our program in a while loop and keep repeating the reading, conversion to Fahrenheit, and displaying of the temperatures. Another option is to press the reset button on the opposite side from the LED grid. That will restart the current program on the micro:bit. I'll make sure I watch more closely to see the current temperature!

Starlight Program

Let's create a relaxing application with our micro:bit. We'll use the grid to randomly display lights at various levels of brightness. Our light grid will show up anytime, but it shows especially well at night or in a dark environment.

Each location in the grid has an (x,y) coordinate pairing. The top left is location (0,0) and the bottom right is (4,4). Here is a table with the grid locations. Notice they do start with 0 for both our rows and columns, just as our index positions do for lists and strings.

(0,0)	(1,0)	(2,0)	(3,0)	(4,0)
(0,1)	(1,1)	(2,1)	(3,1)	(4,1)
(0,2)	(1,2)	(2,2)	(3,2)	(4,2)
(0,3)	(1,3)	(2,3)	(3,3)	(4,3)
(0,4)	(1,4)	(2,4)	(3,4)	(4,4)

Our handy `random.randint()` module can have multiple uses here. We can use it to select our x and y coordinate values for each display. We don't want a pattern here, especially since our eyes are really good at detecting them. It would seem less relaxing if a pattern did exist, too. We can set the start and end values for the random number range, since our grid size is fixed.

```
x = random.randint(0,4)
y = random.randint(0,4)
```

Each LED on our micro:bit has a brightness range, from 1,9. Of course a value of 0 means it is off. We can also use the `random.randint()` module to determine the brightness level of each LED. This also adds variety to our starlight viewing. I'll use a variable named `bright` and set it to a brightness level each time a new LED is set.

```
bright = random.randint(1,9)
```

It's time to display the LED selected at random with our *x* and *y* coordinates and the brightness level! We can use the `while(True):` loop once again to keep our program running to continually display different LED coordinates. We'll also use a new method with our `display()` module: `set_pixel()`. It uses our *x* and *y* coordinates and the brightness level.

```
display.set_pixel(x, y, bright)
```

If we test our program, we see that all the lights are constantly flashing at a rapid rate! This is chaotic and not the relaxing view we had in mind!

Let's think how we can modify this. The `sleep()` method can help us out. With each display of an LED location, we can set how long we want the program to pause before going on to the next `while` loop iteration. You might need to try out a few values for the number of milliseconds you want the program to sleep. I'm going to use 350.

```
sleep(350)
```

Let's download this version to our micro:bit and test it out. It's looking much better (and more relaxing) now. If we keep watching and let it run for a minute or two, do you see an issue with our program? We get to a point where every LED on our grid is on. A slight twinkling effect exists since a position could change from a lower to a higher level of brightness or vice versa, but they're all on to some degree of brightness. This still isn't quite what we imagined.

We have one more modification to make. We need to either periodically clear the entire screen or clear individual LEDs we have turned on before the entire screen turns on. We can add a command to clear the grid after the `sleep(350)` instruction.

```
display.clear()
```

This gets us closer, but only displays one light at a time. It will be displayed for 350 milliseconds, then turned off before the next iteration. The micro:bit processes quickly, so it's okay, but not optimal. Let's add an **if** statement to only clear the screen when the condition is true. We can set the condition to be when *x* equals a particular value, to clear the screen. This keeps some randomness, since we never know when *x* will be that value in any given iteration. We could just as easily use *y* being set to a value as our condition. Pick a value for the condition. Remember, our only options for *x* or *y* are 0, 1, 2, 3, or 4. I'm going to pick 0 for *x*.

```
if (x==0):
  display.clear()
```

So, anytime our random number generator provides 0 for x, then the grid panel will be cleared. It starts right back up filling in new grid values, but it will often display multiple lights before clearing. Here is the complete code.

```
# Star light
from microbit import *
import random

while (True):
  bright = random.randint(1,9)
  x=random.randint(0,4)
  y=random.randint(0,4)
  display.set_pixel(x, y, bright)
  sleep(350)

  if x==0:
    display.clear()
```

I like the look of this random display. Keep tweaking the values and possibilities if you are still not quite happy with it. It's your design!

Guess the Number Game

A micro:bit can also be used for a guessing game. We already know the basic structure from our earlier number guessing games. Let's adapt it for the micro:bit. We will need to give our player some basic instructions since we don't have a keyboard. It can take a while for letters to scroll across the micro:bit, and we don't want the player to miss anything or get bored and stop playing!

We can control the speed that characters are displayed across the micro:bit screen with the `delay = milliseconds` command. This is an option to use with the `display.scroll()` command. It goes after the information to be displayed. I am using 75 milliseconds. Lower numbers were too fast, and higher numbers were too slow. I only want to display the instructions one time, so I make sure these lines of code are outside of any loop we use.

```
display.scroll("text",delay=milliseconds)
```

We can't type in a number or a higher or lower response, but we do have `button_a` and `button_b` that can be used to give us some feedback on our guess. We'll set up this game to have the player think of a number, and we'll program the micro:bit to guess it. We can set the range of numbers to be between 1 and 100, and give the micro:bit 7 guesses to get the right number. We can prompt users for these options:

- Press `button_a` if their number is lower than our guess.

- Press `button_b` if their number is higher than our guess.

- Press both buttons if the guess is correct.

After each button press, we'll need to update the range of numbers used in our guess. If `button_a` is pressed, the number is lower, so we need to keep our lower range the same, and update the high end of the range to be one number less than our previous guess. If our guess was 50, and the player presses `button_a`, we know the number is now between 1–49.

Similarly, if the player presses `button_b` after our guess of 50, we need to update the low end of the range to be one more than our guess. We now know that the number we are trying to guess is between 51 and 100.

With each guess, we also need to decrease our number of guesses by 1. Our `while` loop's condition needs to check that we have not run out of guesses *and* that we have not won the game yet. Inside the `while` loop, we display our guess and then a quick reminder about which button should be pressed. These instructions could get annoying quickly, so it's a shorter version, and I set the delay between letters to be 75 milliseconds. It scrolls pretty quickly.

I then pause the program for a second with the `sleep(1000)` command. This gives the player time to press buttons. If I don't have this, the code runs too quickly and does not always pick up my button press, because I was too slow!

Then, the code checks for which button or buttons were pressed. The order of the conditions is very important here. I first check to see if both buttons were pressed, indicating that the correct number was guessed. If this occurs, then I set `win=True` to stop the loop, and display a smiling face. This condition must be first. Otherwise, if I only checked to see if `button_a` was pressed, it would be true, even if both buttons were being pressed. The fact that `button_b` was pressed would be ignored. The same situation would occur if I checked to see if `button_b` was being pressed to know if my guess was too low. If `button_a` was also being pressed, actually indicating that the correct number was guessed, `button_a` would be ignored.

Remember with an `if/elif` statement, the first condition that is true will have its code run. No other conditions will be checked after one is true, so if our condition to check if the guess is correct is last, it will never be met because either of the two earlier conditions would always be true. Try it out if you're not sure this makes sense.

```
if (button_a.is_pressed()andbutton_b.is_
    pressed()):
    display.show(Image.HAPPY)
    win = True
```

```
elif (button_a.is_pressed()):
  high = guess - 1
elif (button_b.is_pressed()):
  low = guess + 1
```

Finally, we do have to check if we ran out of guesses and lost the game. In this case, a sad face is displayed. Here is the complete program.

```
# Guess number game
from microbit import *
display.scroll("Think of a number between
  1-100.",delay=75)
display.scroll("I can guess the number in 7 or
  fewer guesses.",delay=75)
display.scroll("Press 'A' button if your number
  is lower.",delay=75)
display.scroll("'B' button if number is
  higher.",delay=75)
display.scroll("'A' and 'B' buttons if
  correct!",delay=75)

low = 1
high = 100
numGuesses = 7
win = False
while (numGuesses >0 and win == False):
  guess = int((low + high) / 2)
  display.scroll(guess)
  numGuesses -= 1
  display.scroll("High:A/Low:B or both",delay=75)

  sleep(1000)
```

```
    if (button_a.is_pressed()and button_b.is_
    pressed()):
      display.show(Image.HAPPY)
      win = True
  elif (button_a.is_pressed()):
    high = guess - 1
  elif (button_b.is_pressed()):
    low = guess + 1

  if (numGuesses==0):
      display.show(Image.SAD)
```

Catch the Falling Stars Game

This game requires a little bit of skill. The design includes "falling stars" that can appear in any of the columns on the grid. Each star will start at the top of the grid, and "fall" to the bottom. The player is located in the middle of the bottom row at the start of the round. To move left, the player presses the A button, and to move right, the B button is pressed. The idea is to be in the right position to catch the star to win. If the star gets to the bottom row without being caught, then the player loses that round.

We'll need several variables to make our game work. The player is positioned on the bottom row of the grid. Therefore, the y coordinate will always have the value 4. While we could use a variable for that, we can just code in the value of 4. The player can move anywhere on the row, so the x coordinate can range from 0 to 4. We will need to include a check to be sure we don't try to move outside of that range. The star's y value will always start at 0 since it will always begin at the top of the grid. To make it *fall*, we'll need to keep adding 1 to the y value so it will stay in the right column. We need to make sure we don't try to go past the bottom position for the star's y coordinate, too. The x coordinate for the star will be determined randomly each game. Once calculated, it will stay the same for that round so the star falls straight down.

As usual, we need to provide instructions, but again only once, not at the start of each round. We'll use display statements and have them scroll at 75 milliseconds. It's fast, but not too fast to miss the instructions.

So we can play more than one round at a time, we can use a **while(True)** loop once again. Indented in the loop, we need to display our player in the middle of the bottom row, and start our star falling. Remember with the LED grid, the brightness is the last value in the **set_pixel()** method. We'll keep ours at the highest brightness level of 9.

```
while(True):
    display.set_pixel(bucketx,4,9)
    if (stary<5):
        display.set_pixel(starx,stary,9)
        stary+=1
```

We need to check if either button has been pressed and move the player's position. Don't forget to include the check to be sure we're still in bounds. In my code, if I am still in bounds, I set the brightness of the previous position to be 0, and then update the x value by adding one to move right, or subtracting one to move left and display the new player position. Here's the code for one of the buttons.

```
if (button_a.is_pressed()):
    if (bucketx-1 >= 0):
        display.set_pixel(bucketx,4,0)
        bucketx-=1
        display.set_pixel(bucketx,4,9)
```

Our last step is to see if the star fell all the way by reaching the bottom row, which has a y value of 4. If our player's y coordinate is also 4, and their x coordinate is also the same, then we caught the star and display the heart image. If the player's x value is not the same, a sad face is displayed. In both cases, we're ready to start a new game, so we need to reset all our values. Since this code would be duplicated, it gives us the opportunity to define our own function and call it either time we need it. I called mine `reset()`.

Remember that functions must be defined before they can be called in a program, so we'll put it at the top, after the import statements. One important factor to remember is that we are *changing* the values of our player and star coordinates. Therefore, we need to declare these as global variables in our function. Otherwise, a local variable with the same name is created and we'll be very confused about how our program then begins to work. Here's the complete code.

```
# Catch the Falling Stars Game
from microbit import *
import random

def reset():
    global starx, stary, bucketx
    starx = random.randint(0,4)
    stary = 0
    bucketx = 2
    sleep(500)
    display.clear()

bucketx = 2
starx = random.randint(0,4)
stary = 0

display.scroll("Move the bottom row bucket to
    catch the falling stars!",delay=75)
display.scroll("Press Button A to move left",
    delay=75)
display.scroll("or Button B to move right",
    delay=75)
```

```
while(True):
  display.set_pixel(bucketx,4,9)
  if (stary<5):
      display.set_pixel(starx,stary,9)
      stary+=1


  if (button_a.is_pressed()):

      if (bucketx-1 >= 0):
          display.set_pixel(bucketx,4,0)
          bucketx-=1
          display.set_pixel(bucketx,4,9)

  if (button_b.is_pressed()):

      if (bucketx+1 <= 4):
          display.set_pixel(bucketx,4,0)
          bucketx+=1
          display.set_pixel(bucketx,4,9)

  if (stary==4 and starx==bucketx):
      display.show(Image.HEART)
      reset()
  elif (stary==4 and starx != bucketx):
      display.show(Image.SAD)
      reset()

  sleep(300)
```

Your reflexes are probably better than mine, so you may decide that the delay provided by the **sleep()** function is too long. Change the number of milliseconds for the delay to make it challenging for you and your friends!

You also might want to change the images displayed when you catch the star (the heart) or miss it (the sad face). Have fun with it!

Make Your Own Music

One of the great things about the micro:bit is that people are creating and sharing new modules. One of these is a music library. We'll need to import this library since it does not come with the micro:bit. No problem! We pull it into our program just as we did the random library using the `import` command. We need to import it before we can reference any modules in the library, so be sure to place the import statement just after the `from microbit import *` line.

The music library includes quite a few songs and a command to play them. The `music.play()` command must be used. The library name is music and `play()` is a method in the music library. Inside the parentheses, we provide the library name and the file in the library to play.

Here is the code to import the music library and play a fanfare called music.DADADADUM.

```
# Play music
from microbit import *
import music
music.play(music.DADADADUM)
```

If you try it on your micro:bit, you won't hear anything! You might think the program has an error because nothing happens. At least nothing happens that we can detect. We have to set up a way to hear the music. I always include a `display` statement to show a music note in my program, so I know that it is working while I get my speakers or headphones set up. Try adding this to your program before the line to play the music:

```
display.show(Image.MUSIC_QUAVER)
```

To be able to hear the music from the micro:bit, we need to use two alligator clips to connect speakers or headphones to the micro:bit. Note: If you do not have alligator clips, you can use aluminum foil and scotch tape. Connect one end of an alligator clip to the GND or ground circle on the bottom right of the micro:bit. Connect one end of the other alligator clip to pin 0 on the bottom left of the micro:bit. If you are using foil, take a piece and fold it over to look like a wire. Tape it to the GND pin. Be sure there is a good connection. Repeat this process with another section of foil and then tape it to pin 0.

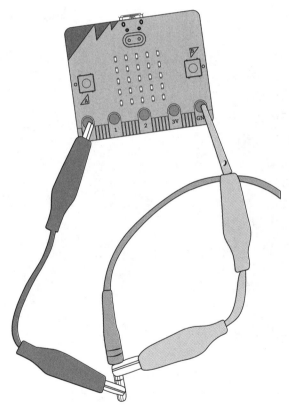

Then, take the other end of the alligator clip, or foil, that is connected to the GND pin and connect it to the base of the headphone or speaker jack. Now, connect the other end of the pin 0 clip or foil to the tip of the speaker jack. Now, when we run our music program on the micro:bit, we have a way to hear the music! Try out the different songs. Here is the list of available songs in the library:

```
music.DADADADUM
music.ENTERTAINER
music.PRELUDE
music.ODE
music.NYAN
music.RINGTONE
music.FUNK
music.BLUES
music.BIRTHDAY
music.WEDDING
music.FUNERAL
music.PUNCHLINE
music.PYTHON
music.BADDY
music.CHASE
music.BA_DING
music.WAWAWAWAA
music.JUMP_UP
music.JUMP_DOWN
music.POWER_UP
music.POWER_DOWN
```

We can play multiple songs from the library. One way would be to start playing a song, and then use buttons A and B to switch between two additional songs. In this code, I added a `sleep()` function to give me time to press a button before the code checked for that condition. I also added different images to display when the buttons were pressed. Here's the code for this.

```
# Play music
from microbit import *

import music
display.show(Image.MUSIC_QUAVER)
music.play(music.ENTERTAINER)
sleep(1000)
if (button_a.is_pressed()):
  display.show(Image.YES)
  music.play(music.DADADADUM)
elif (button_b.is_pressed()):
  display.show(Image.NO)
  music.play(music.WAWAWAWAA)
```

You can set up different scenarios to switch between songs or build a list and select which one to play at random. With the list, you can also set up a `while` or `for loop` to play each one in a playlist.

Follow the Leader Game

This game will challenge us to repeat a pattern provided by the micro:bit. We'll "follow the leader" to see if we can remember all the steps. We will use the left and right direction arrows that come with the image library to point to the moves the player should make. The player will use button A to indicate a left-pointing arrow and button B for a right-pointing arrow.

We will need to generate random integers to create our pattern each time. Therefore, we'll import the `random` library.

```
# Follow the Leader Game
from microbit import *
import random
```

These are the variables needed. I'm using three lists. One will hold the new **pattern** created randomly each round. Another list will hold the player **response**. I added a *count* variable to make it easier for slow players (like me) to get their button presses included in the player moves list. The **directions** list holds the arrows used in the game and the pattern is generated from these.

```
count = 0
pattern = []
response = []
directions = [Image.ARROW_E, Image.ARROW_W]
```

This **for** loop is used to create the opening pattern and store it in the **pattern** list. We have a new built-in function, **range()** to determine the number of iterations for our loop. The **range()** function takes an integer as an argument. It then creates a "range" of numbers from 0 up to but not including the number provided. I want to generate a pattern of 3 arrows, so I use 3 as the argument, and my loop runs 3 times. Inside the loop, a random number for the index is generated. The index is for the **directions** list. Since we have two elements, the East and West arrows, the two index positions can only be 0 or 1, but are repeated multiple times.

```
for i in range(3):
  pattern.append(directions[random.randint(0,1)])
```

This **for** loop shows the pattern to the player.

```
for i in range(len(pattern)):
  display.show(pattern[i])
  sleep(500)
  display.clear()
```

The *" : "* in the *display.scroll()* statement below shows the user that the pattern is over, and it's time for them to demonstrate how good their memory and reflexes are!

```
display.scroll(":")
```

This **while** loop iterates as many times as the number of elements in the pattern. It increases the counter and displays it so the player knows which move they are repeating. The button that the player presses causes the East- or West-facing arrow to be added to the **responses** list.

```
while (count < len(pattern)):
    count+=1
    display.show(str(count))

    if (button_a.is_pressed()):
        response.append(directions[1])

    elif (button_b.is_pressed()):
        response.append(directions[0])
```

The moves that the player made are then displayed back to them using a **for** loop. The loop will display each element in the list after a slight delay.

```
for i in range(len(response)):
    display.show(response[i])
    sleep(750)
```

The contents of the pattern list are compared to the player response list. If they match, the check mark image is shown, and if they do not, then a big "X" is displayed.

```
if (response==pattern):
  display.show(Image.YES)
else:
  display.show(Image.NO)
```

Here is the final code. I added several **sleep()** commands to slow down the micro:bit's processing so the player has time to see the pattern and make a move.

```
# Follow the Leader Game
from microbit import *
import random

count = 0
pattern = []
response = []
directions = [Image.ARROW_E, Image.ARROW_W]

# Create the opening pattern
for i in range(3):
  pattern.append(directions[random.randint(0,1)])

# Display the pattern for the player
for i in range(len(pattern)):
    display.show(pattern[i])
    sleep(500)
    display.clear()

display.scroll(":")
sleep(1000)

# Append player moves to response list
while (count < len(pattern)):
```

```
    count+=1
    display.show(str(count))
    sleep(750)
    if (button_a.is_pressed()):
      response.append(directions[1])

    elif (button_b.is_pressed()):
      response.append(directions[0])

display.clear()
sleep(1000)
# Display player moves
for i in range(len(response)):
  display.show(response[i])
  sleep(750)
  display.clear()

# Compare results
if (response==pattern):
  display.show(Image.YES)
else:
  display.show(Image.NO)

sleep(1000)
```

This is a fun game where timing is key to winning a round or losing! You can modify the program to create a longer pattern. You can set it to a certain length of your choosing or ask the player how many moves to include in their challenge. There are lots of options to keep it interesting.

We have covered a lot of material, from the basics of Python to using a subset of it with the micro:bit. There is far more you can do with both Python and the micro:bit. I encourage you to explore, research, and keep programming with both Python 3 and microPython with the micro:bit. You'll be amazed at the things you can now do as a programmer. Congratulations!

Flashcard
App

Answer Key

1
Hardware and Software

1. a. Input
   b. Output
   c. CPU
   d. Memory
2. Through ports on the motherboard
3. Holds the instructions and data that are running in memory.
4. When the power is turned off, whatever was currently stored in RAM is not retained.
5. The "brain" of the computer

2
A Computer's Favorite Language — Binary!

1. It is easy to determine if there is current or no current going through the circuits. These two options provide a way to build logic gates that produce true or false outcomes.
2. Short for binary digit. It can hold the value 0 or 1.
3. 8 bits.

4. Place value with binary works the same as with decimal numbers but uses the number 2 as the base rather than 10. Each bit in a binary number is represented by 2 raised to a power starting with 2^0 in the far right or 1s column. Rather than ones, tens, hundreds and so on with the decimal number system, we have ones, twos, fours, eights, and so on with the binary number system.

5. Let's build our "power of 2s" table.

2^7	2^6	2^5	2^4	2^3	2^2	2^1	2^0
128	64	32	16	8	4	2	1

We need to find the largest value we can subtract from 23 without ending up with a negative number. That will be 16 in this example. Therefore, we need to put a 1 in the 16s column and 0 in the columns to the left of it.

2^7	2^6	2^5	2^4	2^3	2^2	2^1	2^0
128	64	32	16	8	4	2	1
0	0	0	1				

$$23 - 16 = 7$$

Now we repeat these steps and find the next largest number to subtract from 7 without a negative difference. 8 is too large, so a 0 goes in that column. A 4 is the next number we can use, so a 1 goes in the 4s column.

$$7 - 4 = 3$$

Now we can subtract 2, so we place a 1 in the 2s column.

$$3 - 2 = 1$$

And we finally subtract $1 - 1 = 0$ and place a 1 in that column.

2^7	2^6	2^5	2^4	2^3	2^2	2^1	2^0
128	64	32	16	8	4	2	1
0	0	0	1	0	1	1	1

$00010111_2 = 23_{10}$

6. Let's build our "power of 2s" table.

2^7	2^6	2^5	2^4	2^3	2^2	2^1	2^0
128	64	32	16	8	4	2	1
0	1	1	1	1	0	0	1

We need to find the largest value we can subtract from 121 without ending up with a negative number. That will be 64 in this example. Therefore, we need to put a 1 in the 64s column, and 0 in the 128s column to the left of it.

$121 - 64 = 57$

The next number we can subtract is 32, so place a 1 in the 32s columns.

$57 - 32 = 25$

We can subtract 16, so place a 1 in the 16s column.

$25 - 16 = 9$

We can subtract 8, so a 1 goes in that column.

$9 - 8 = 1$

We cannot subtract 4 or 2 from 1 and have a positive result, so 0 goes in both those columns.

We finish with $1 - 1 = 0$ and place a 1 in the 1s column.

$01111001_2 = 121_{10}$

7.

2^7	2^6	2^5	2^4	2^3	2^2	2^1	2^0
128	64	32	16	8	4	2	1
0	1	1	0	0	0	1	1

We need to find the largest value we can subtract from 99 without ending up with a negative number. That will be 64 in this example. Therefore, we need to put a 1 in the 64s column, and 0 in the 128s column to the left of it.

$$99 - 64 = 35$$

We can subtract 32, so a 1 goes in that column.

$$35 - 32 = 3$$

We cannot subtract 16, 8, or 4 and end up with a positive number, so 0 goes in those columns. We can subtract 2, so place a 1 in the 2s columns.

$$3 - 2 = 1$$

We end with $1 - 1 = 0$ and place a 1 in the 1s column.

$$01100011_2 = 99_{10}$$

8. In this case, we can start with our table and load this binary number into each column.

2^7	2^6	2^5	2^4	2^3	2^2	2^1	2^0
128	64	32	16	8	4	2	1
0	1	0	1	0	0	1	1

We are essentially multiplying the binary value by the 2 power and adding them together. Since 0 times any number is 0, we don't need to write those out.

$$1 \times 2^6 + 1 \times 2^4 + 1 \times 2^1 + 1 \times 2^0$$
$$64 + 16 + 2 + 1 = 83_{10}$$

9. Let's load this binary number into each column.

2^7	2^6	2^5	2^4	2^3	2^2	2^1	2^0
128	64	32	16	8	4	2	1
0	1	1	0	1	0	1	1

$$64 + 32 + 8 + 2 + 1 = 107_{10}$$

10. Load this binary number into each column.

2^7	2^6	2^5	2^4	2^3	2^2	2^1	2^0
128	64	32	16	8	4	2	1
1	1	0	0	0	0	1	1

$$128 + 64 + 2 + 1 = 195_{10}$$

Getting Started

1. Machine language, which is binary

2. A compiler or interpreter translates the programming language that people use to machine code.

3. Compilers translate the entire code and create an executable file. Interpreters translate a program to machine code line by line.

4. A compiler executes faster than an interpreter because it processes an entire program to machine code all at once. Since the interpreter goes line by line, there is additional time to fetch each line.

5. A software development process helps us ensure we fully understand the requirements our code needs to produce, that we create a well thought-out design to meet those requirements, document it, and, after coding, we fully test our code before releasing it for widespread use.

6. The process of breaking down the requirements for a program into manageable sections. The sections can be broken down several times before getting to the point of writing code for a section. The sections are then integrated into the final programming solution.

7. An iterative process allows us to develop smaller units of code, test and rework them as needed in additional iterations, and then build another set in the next iteration.

8. This is where the algorithm for the solution is figured out. More time spent producing a good design in this phase will result in less time spent in other phases. A good design ensures features were not missed and have to be retro fit in later, which can produce less efficient, less readable, and less maintainable code.

9. Unit testing is when the programmer tries to find all errors before having others test the code.

10. Testing all the modules involved in a programming feature to be sure they correctly work together.

Designing a Programming Solution: Algorithms

1. A set of steps to do something

2. Algorithms are not written in a programming language, although elements of a programming language can be and often are used. Algorithms are generic and could be implemented in any programming language.

3. Computers cannot infer what we mean as a person can when instructions are unclear. We have to be very precise in describing algorithms for a computer to ensure the expected result occurs.

4. Your solution may be different than this, but the overall concept should be the same.

> Open computer screen
>
> Type in password (or swipe fingerprint)
>
> If typed in incorrect password (or band aid on finger)
>
>> Try to type in password
>
> If correct password or (fingerprint)
>
>> Open screen to last screen used
>
> If password wrong too many times
>
>> Lock the screen

5. Your steps may differ from these and still be correct.
   1. Draw 2 parallel lines about 2 inches long 3 inches apart.
   2. Draw a line connecting them at the bottom.
   3. Draw a line from the center of the bottom line down 3 inches.
   4. Done!

6. Suggestions could include:
   1. Size of the circles?
   2. Where should the two circles be in relation to each other, beside each other?
   3. How should the circles be connected?
   4. How big of a "round thing" should be drawn on each side?
   5. Should the "round thing" be on both sides of both circles?
   6. Is the hump at the top of the circles or the top of the page?

The drawing is supposed to be of headphones!

Pseudocode and Flowcharts

1. Part English/part programming language. Pseudocode cannot run on a computer, as it is not a complete programming language solution.

2. Helps a programmer design a solution for the algorithm prior to coding.

3. Computers cannot run pseudocode as it is not a pure programming language that a compiler or interpreter could translate to binary. It is a combination of English and some code to help set up the structure of a program.

4. To help programmers design solutions before starting to code. Some people prefer the diagram over the pseudocode.

5. The shapes used with flowcharts have designated meanings. This helps others to better understand a flowchart and the program structure and purpose. Specific shapes with the correct meaning should be used. The shapes are included in many software programs, including Microsoft Word and Google Docs.

6. Your solution will probably look different from this, and can still be correct.

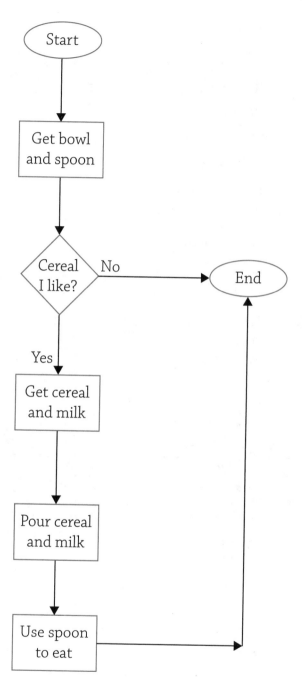

7. Your solution will be different from this, and may still be correct.

Check if vending machine has item wanted

If yes, insert money

> # Calculate if owe more money, paid too much, or exact amount paid
>
> If owe more money,
>
>> Prompt user how much more to insert
>
> If paid too much
>
>> Calculate and release change
>>
>> Vend item
>
> Else
>
>> Vend item

8. Your solution will be different from this, and may still be correct.

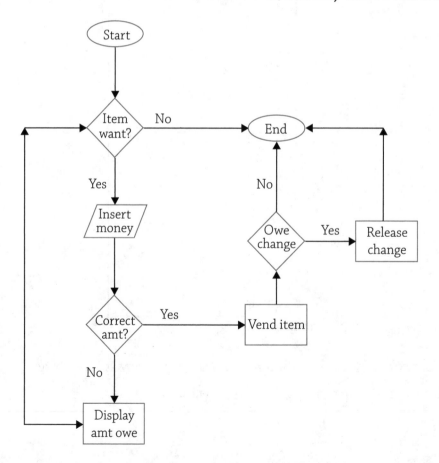

Writing and Commenting
Our First Program

1. Integrated Development Environment

2. Allows programmers to write, test, document, and modify code. IDEs include built-in compilers and interpreters, along with debugging tools to help the software developers.

3. `print("text")`

   The `print()` command is used and text fields are wrapped in quotation marks.

4. Python displays what is included within the parentheses of the `print()` command.

5. Shown in color

6. You cannot mix single and double quotation marks. Both can be used, but the same format must be used for the opening and the closing quotation marks for the same field.

7. The prompt has the >>> symbols, indicating we are in the Python shell window.

8. .py

9. scripts

10. `print("your name")`

11. `print("My pet is named: pet name")`

12. To describe the purpose of the program; to describe important or complex sections of code

13. The # symbol

14. You use triple quotation marks at the beginning of the block and at the end of it.

    """

Comments

" " "

Three single quotation marks (apostrophe) can also be used.

15. Your comments will be different, but should be similar.

    # Turns on a coffeepot based on the day of the week.

    # On weekdays, the coffeepot is started at 6:00 a.m.

    # On weekends, the coffeepot is started at 8:00 a.m.

Debugging and Testing

1. The process of removing errors from our code

2. To be sure it is handled without making our program crash. Someone will inevitably use invalid data, so we need to handle those cases with our code.

3. A boundary value is one on either side of a condition that is being used. These should be tested to be sure our program does not process one too few or one too many cases.

4. Part of good testing is to determine the expected result from a given input. Then we know for certain if our program works correctly for that type of data input.

5. You may have some of these or additional tests that are equally correct.

    1. Test for an integer input for temperature.

    2. Test using a float (decimal number) input.

    3. Test for a text field input.

    4. Test to ensure the conversion calculation is correct.

6. A runtime error

7. A syntax error

8. A logic error

9. a. Syntax error. The **print()** command is written with all lowercase letters.

   b. Syntax error. The quotation marks are mixed with a single quotation mark at the beginning and a double quotation mark at the end.

   c. Syntax error. The **print()** command uses parentheses, not braces.

Variables and Assignment Statements

1. a. This is a valid variable name and uses camelCase to make the variable name easier to read.

   b. This is invalid because it starts with a number.

   c. This is invalid because it has a symbol, #, as part of the variable name.

   d. This is invalid because it has a space in the name. Python will think it is two variable names.

2. Variable names should describe the data they hold. The variable name, *asdf*, does not describe anything and is not a good variable name.

3. There are several options that would be good variable names. Here are a couple of options.

   snack

   favSnack

4. There are several options that would be good variable names. Here are a few options.

   music

   myMusic

   myFavMusic

5. Here are several possible options.

   address

   addr

   home

   homeAddr

   mailingAddress

6. A single equals sign is used: =

7. Yes, a variables value can be changed as often as needed.

8. Yes, a variable can be used in a calculation to determine the value to assign a different variable.

9. Your variable names may be different, but should still be descriptive.

   `myTeamGames = numGames`

10. Your variable names may be different, but should still be descriptive.

    `winPercent = numWins / numLosses`

11. This example should be similar to yours. Your variable names may be different, but should still be descriptive. You may have more than two streaks included in your calculation.

    `snapChatStreakAvg = (streak1 + streak2) / numStreaks`

12. `testScore = 92`

    `extraCredit = 5`

    `testScore = testScore + extraCredit`

    `print(testScore)`

    97 is printed.

    This takes the current value of testScore, which is 92, adds the current value of extraCredit to it, which becomes 92 + 5. This new value of 97 is then stored back into testScore. The previous value of 92 is gone and cannot be retrieved.

13. ```
numberOfPlayers = 0
numberOfPlayers = numberOfPlayers + 1
```

Note: You could also write this as

```
numberOfPlayers += 1
```

14. ```
noShows = numRegistered
noShows = noShows — 1
```

You could also write this as
```
noShows -= 1
```

15. ```
print("Number of registrations:", numRegistered,
"\n\tNumber of Players:", numberOfPlayers,
"\n\tNumber registered that did not attend:",
noShows)
```

16. ```
print("Number of registrations:", "{:,}".
format(numRegistered), "\n\tNumber of Players:",
"{:,}".format(numberOfPlayers),
"\n\tNumber registered that did not attend:",
"{:,}".format(noShows))
```

17. ```
print("The average of the three scores is: {:.3f}"
.format((test1 + test2 + test3)/3))
```

# Data Types

1. float

2. 0 and −999 are the only integers in the list.

3. strings

4. Use quotation marks around the field to make it a string.
   It has the data type: str.
```

5. −0.5, −1.0, 0.0, and 5432.1 are all floats because they all have decimals. Even if the number after the decimal point is 0, it is still a float.

6. ```
pet = "dog"
```

7. ```
name = "my name"
```

8. The decimal and the numbers after the decimal point are truncated or lopped off.

9. No. Since the 440 symbols look like numbers, they can be converted to a float value. The value stored in memory will be 440.0.

10. This will cause an error since the address includes numbers and letters. The letters cannot be converted to integers.

11. ```
locker = 123
locker = str(locker)
print(locker)
```

    You could also use a different variable name to hold the converted string value.

    ```
lockerList = str(locker)
print(lockerList)
```

12. In programming, truncate means to lop off the decimal and any numbers after it. There is no rounding of the whole number either up nor down.

    The result is only the whole number that existed before the truncation.

13. When a float is cast to be an integer

14. The `type()` function determines the data type of a variable name placed inside the parentheses.

15. ```
numThrows = 0
print(numThrows)
print(type(numThrows))
```

16. str. The quotation marks tell Python that the value is a string.

17. float. Since age is "18" from the first line of code, converting it to a float in line 2 will change the value to be 18.0.

18. integer. The decimal and any decimal values will be truncated. If we keep with our example of 18.0, when we convert it to be an integer, the .0 is truncated and the value 18 is stored in the variable age.

The variable *age* had three different data types in this example. It started as a string, then we converted it to be a real number (with a decimal), and finally it was converted to be an integer. Python handled converting the data type for the variable *age* in each case.

Math Symbols

1. Addition   +

   Subtraction   −

   Multiplication *

   Division   /

   Exponent   **

2. When a float is cast to an int, the decimal portion will be truncated.

```
num1 = 2.5
num2 = int(num1)
print(num2)
2                          # This is the output printed
```

3. ```testAvg = (test1 + test2 + test3) / 3```

4. ```numPizzas = (5 * 3) / 8```

5. No! Only the / (forward slash) symbol is used for division.

   Remember that the back slash is used with our escape characters when printing string output.

6. `calc = 2**3`

   This is the same as writing 2 * 2 * 2. The value of *calc* is 8.

7. `%`

8. Only the remainder after dividing is kept as the result.

9. `hour = 7`

   `time1 = hour % 12`

   We divide hour, which is 7, by 12. We get 0 as the quotient and 7 as the remainder. Only the 7 is kept with modulus math.

       `time1 = 7`

10. `hour = 18`

    `time2 = hour % 12`

    We divide hour, which is 18, by 12. We get 1 as the quotient and 6 as the remainder. Only the 6 is returned with modulus math.

        `time2 = 6`

11. `evenOdd = number % 2`

    If our variable *evenOdd*'s value is 1, then we know it is an odd number.

    If the variable is *0*, then it is an even number.

12. `threes = number % 3`

13. If the value stored in the variable *threes* is 0, then the number is divisible by 3.

    `num = 1.0 * (17 / 3) - 2`

    Using the order of operations, the (17/3) will be calculated first due to the parentheses.

    Next, 1.0 will be multiplied by the result of (17/3).

    Finally, 2 will be subtracted from that value.

    The answer is:

        3.66667

14.
```
radius = 4
pi = 3.14
circumference = 2 * pi * radius
print(circumference)
```

15.
```
shoeSize = 7
yearBorn = 1999
answer = (((shoeSize * 5) + 50) * 20) + 1020 - \
  yearBorn
print(answer)
```

Note that the \ is used as a continuation character because this line of code could not fit all on one line. When you type this code into your program, you will not need the continuation character and should leave it out. Otherwise, you will get a syntax error.

The first digit of the variable *answer* should be your shoe size, and the next digit or digits should be your age (unless you've already had a birthday this year).

Strings

1.
```
artist = "One hit wonder"
print(artist[5])
```

The letter i would be printed. The index positions start with 0. The index position 5 holds the letter i.

value	O	n	e		h	i	t		w	o	n	d	e	r
index	0	1	2	3	4	5	6	7	8	9	10	11	12	13

2.
```
print(artist[72 - 68])
```

This is equivalent to artist[4]. The 72−68 calculation will be performed first.

Then the letter at index position 4 is found and printed.

The letter h will be printed.

3. `print(artist[-3])`

This is a valid index position. It starts with the length of our string, which is 14.

You can type `print(len(artist))` in Python to confirm this.

We take 14 − 3 to calculate the index position, which will be 11.

The letter at index position 11 is d.

4. `print(artist[len(artist) — 1])`

This uses the *len()* built-in function to find the length of the variable *artist*, subtracts one from the length to get a valid index position, and then prints the character at that index location. It is the last letter in our string, which is r.

5. Write some index position examples of your own. Type them into Python to confirm your result.

6. `song = "do re mi "`

`print(song + song)`

With strings, the + sign signals concatenation, which glues strings together.

The following string will be printed:

> do re mi do re mi

7. `song = "do re mi "`

`print(song * 3)`

With strings, the multiplication sign, *, will cause the string to be duplicated the indicated number of times. Here song will be printed 3 times.

> do re mi do re mi do re mi

8. We concatenate using the plus sign, +.

     fullName = firstName + middleName + lastName

     (Yes, this was a joke!)

9. Immutable means unchangeable.

10. In Python, a copy of the string with the change is made and stored in memory. The new changed string is then used.

11. With slicing, the first number is inclusive, but the second one is exclusive.

     Therefore, we want the characters from index position 0–7. The answer is:

     Coding i

12. When no value is provided for the first position, Python will start at the beginning, which is index position 0. This slice includes 0–12 or:

     Coding is awe

13. This slice goes from 13 to 16 since the second number is up to but not including 17 or:

     some

14. When a value is not provided for the second position in the slice, Python will go to the end of the variable. This slice includes 15–17 or:

     me!

15. This combines several concepts to determine our slice. For the starting index position, Python will first have to calculate the length of our string variable and then subtract 8 from it. This value is (18 – 8) or 10. Since our ending slice location goes beyond the end of the string, it will include the rest of the characters in the string. Our answer is:

     awesome!

16. The **find()** method will provide the index position of the character if it finds it or −1 if it does not. The letter a is in our string twice. If a character is in a string more than once, the **find()** method will return the first occurrence of a string. This one returns:

     5

17. The `lower()` method will convert the string to all lowercase and return a copy of it with the changes, since strings are immutable.

    fire alarm test

18. `alert.replace("test", "drill")`

19. `continue.startswith("y")` will check if the user's response begins with a lowercase y.

Input

1. Otherwise, their response from the keyboard is lost in cyberspace and you cannot retrieve it to use later in the program.

2. Pauses the program and waits for input from the keyboard. As soon as the *Enter* key is detected, the function will capture whatever was typed.

3. The user will need to know what type of input the program needs, so we can put a message inside the parentheses of the `input()` function.

   `guess = input("Guess a number between 1-10")`

4. The *try:* section gives us a chance to test lines of code, such as user input, and the *except:* provides a way to avoid crashing the program if there is an error in the try: section.

5. Indentation is critical in Python as it is used to indicate code that is associated with the statement it is indented under.

6. The `except:` command and any code associated with it executes only when an error occurs in the try: section.

7. No. You also cannot have a *try:* without an *except:* statement. These two travel together.

8. A colon, :, must be after both the *try:* and *except:* statements.

9. Can be used to indicate an event occurred. For example, the flag variable can be set to a certain value in the *except:* code when an error

was detected in the *try:* section. The program can check for the flag variable's value to determine if additional processing should occur.

10. Your answer will differ from this, but should provide the same functionality.

```
temp = input("What is the current temperature? ")
try:
    # convert the string value to a float
    temp = float(temp)
except:
    print("An error occurred. Temperature values
    must be numbers.")
```

11. A flag variable should be set in the *except:* section of code so that the program continues processing. Certain operations are not tested since an error occurred.

```
flag = "y"
```

12. The code is correct, but remember that indentation is very important to Python. The lines of code underneath the *try:* statement and the lines underneath the *except:* must be indented for the program to run.

```
age = input("Please enter your age: ")
try:
    age = int(age)
except:
    print("Error: Age must be a whole number.")
    flag = 1
```

13. Links a file to our program for use. While our program has the file open, other programs cannot use it.

14. Allows the program to write to a file. Any data already in the file will be overwritten. If the file does not already exist, it will automatically be created.

15. Write mode will overwrite anything that is already in a file.

Append will write new data at the end of existing data. Append does not overwrite data that is already there.

16. `with open("temp.txt", "r") as fileIn:`

The first value inside the parentheses is the file name.

The second value is the mode to open the file. The r stands for read only mode. Your filename and file handle may be different but the rest of the statement should be the same.

13

Three Types of Statements

1. Selection statement. It includes a condition to evaluate. If the condition is true, the code indented under the "if" will be executed.

2. The repetitive statement or loop runs a block of code multiple times.

3. Sequential statement

14

Selection Statements

1. a. Yes, since there are only two options, it can be set for heads to be true and tails to be false (or vice versa.)

   b. Yes, since there are only two possibilities for the lights, it can be set up as a Boolean. Lights on can be true and lights off can be false (or vice versa.)

   c. Since the options for this question are yes or no, this can be used as a Boolean using yes for true and no for false. Around my house, my answer would always be yes, but my children would always say no!

d. This cannot be used as a Boolean condition since there are seven possibilities for the day of the week. Booleans only have two possibilities, true or false.

2. Here is one possible solution.

```
sibling = input("Do you have a sibling? 'y' or 'n'
if (sibling == "y"):
    print("You are lucky you have a sibling!")
```

3. Here is one possible solution.

```
whistle = input("Can you whistle? 'y' or 'n'")
if (whistle == "y"):
    print("You can whistle! I can too!")
```

4. >

5. <=. You write the combination in the order that we say it, so the less than symbol comes before the equal sign.

6. For comparison with conditionals since a single equals sign is used to assign a value to a variable.

7. Here is one possible solution.

```
favoriteSong = "your favorite here"
if (song == favoriteSong):
    print("This is my favorite song!")
```

8. A colon must be at the end of the condition section of an *if* statement.

9. Parentheses are not required for Python's *if* statement. However, many other programming languages do require it, so it is a good habit to get into anyway.

10. We must indent any code to be executed when a condition is true one level (or one tab) underneath the condition.

11.
```
if (day == "Saturday" or day == "Sunday"):
    alarm = "off"
else:
    alarm = "0600"
```

This could also be written as:

```
if (day == "Monday" or day == "Tuesday" or day
  == "Wednesday" or day == "Thursday" or day ==
  "Friday"):
  alarm = "0600"
else:
  alarm = "off"
```

12.
```
lake = True
if (lake == True):
   print("Wash dogs!")
```

You could also write this condition as below. It reads as: "if True"

```
if (lake):
   print("Wash dogs!")
```

13. This tests if the price of an item is $100 or more.

14. This tests whether someone was on time for the bus and caught it.

    The condition could also have been written as:

```
if (onTime == True):
```

15.
```
if (listen):
    playSong()
else:
    skipSong()
```

16.
```
if (feet == "hurt" or shoes == "worn"):
    print("Go buy new shoes!")
```

17. If a condition is false, the code associated with it will *not* execute.

18. When a line of code is unindented back to the same level as the *if* condition, Python knows that the code associated with a selection statement is finished.

19. This pseudocode is testing if it is time to feed the dog.

   If it is 6:00 p.m. (or 1800), then the dog is fed.

   The dog is played with and brushed even if it is not 6:00 p.m. because those statements are not indented under the *if* statement.

20. No. Python will keep checking conditions until one of them is true. Then, no other conditions will be checked.

21. Python will only execute the code with the first true condition it finds.

22. The phrase, "Check the rule book" will be printed.

23.
```
if (num % 3 == 0):
    num = num + 10
elif (num % 3 == 1):
    num = num + 5
```

24. Since the first five characters are the same in both strings, the comparison is actually done on the "E" and "S". Based on this, the output is:

   Shelve Jane Eyre first.

25. The colon is missing after both the *if* and the *else* statements.

   The relational operator is in the wrong order. It should be $>=$ for greater than or equal to.

15
Logical Operators

1. A compound condition that uses *or* is true whenever either or both conditions are true.

2. A compound condition that uses *and* is false whenever one or both conditions are false.

3. When it is 5:00 p.m. and it is not raining.

4. If it is Saturday at 1:00 p.m.

5. Nothing is printed here because both of the conditions are not true. The condition for (book2 <= book1) is false, so the entire condition will be false regardless of whether book3 < book2 (which it is.)

6. Your variables will be different, but the structure should be the same.

```
if (musicTaste == "classic rock" and playGuitar):
```

You could also write this as:

```
if (musicTaste == "classic rock" and playGuitar
== True):
```

7. Your variables will be different, but the structure should be the same.

```
if ((day == "Saturday" or day == "Sunday") and
daysClean > 10):
```

8. "The coffeepot is not turned on."

The condition is false because the time given is 7:00 p.m. or 1900, not 7:00 a.m.

Also, the day is Wednesday and this part of the condition is true when it is Monday.

9. This is one possible solution.

```
if (time >= 2100):    # Tests for 9:00 p.m.
# or later
    watchTV == True
```

10.
```
if (collegeRank <= 50 and collegePublic ==
True):
    print("Apply!")
```
You could also write this as:
```
if (collegeRank <= 50 and collegePublic):
```

11. This code tests if the player still has lives. The game will continue if this is true. Otherwise, the message displayed will ask if they want to play the game again, because they have no more lives and the game is over.

12.
```
if (movieToSee == True and money < 15):
    print("Ask for chores to earn money")
else:
    print("Go to movie!")
```
You could also write this as:
```
if (movieToSee and money < 15):
```

13.
```
# Still have challenges to solve if challenges > 0
if (not(challenges > 0)):
    print("Time to level up!")
```

14.
```
if (win and score > highestScore):
    highestScore = score
    print("You have the new high score!")
```

16

Lists

1.
```
movies = ["Star Wars", "Gone with the Wind",
"Color Purple"]
```

2. You will have actual values in your example.

```
me = ["name", "height", "age", "eye color"]
```

3. Elements

4. We use the index position to access an individual item in a list.

5. 0

6. Your choices will vary!

```
favFood = ["popcorn", "pizza", "strawberries",
    "cucumbers"]
print(favFood)
favFood[1] = "veggie soup"
print(favFood)
```

7.
```
numScores = len(scores)
print(numScores, scores[numScores - 1])
```

This could also be written as:

```
print(len(scores), scores[len(scores) - 1])
```

8. # Your list will have actual song names in it

```
favSongs = ["song1", "song2", "song3", "song4",
    "song5"]
for song in favSongs:
  if (len(song) % 2 == 0):
    print(song)
print("Play it again!")
```

9. a. Append the next two values in the Fibonacci series to the list.

```
fibonacci.append(21)
```

```
fibonacci.append(34)
```

b. Print your Fibonacci list to confirm the values.

```
for num in fibonacci:
    print(num)
```

10.
```
roster.insert(5, "John Quincy Adams")
for pres in roster:
  print(pres)
```

The output of printing the list now should be:

Washington

Adams

Jefferson

Madison

Monroe

John Quincy Adams

Jackson

Van Buren

11. `pets.remove("horse")`

12. `pets.pop(4)`

13. `del pets[4]`

or

`pets.remove("snake")`

14.
```
Start with the first element as the largest
# number for num in weights:
large = weights
for num in weights: [0]
    if (num > large):
        large = num
print("The largest number in the list is:",
large)
```

15. 90.3 is displayed.

16. 180.6 is displayed

17. 45.15 is displayed.

18. 88.3 is displayed

19. [42, 256, 1023, 42, 256, 1023, 42, 256, 1023] is displayed.

Repetitive Statements: *while* Loops

1. When the variable tested in the condition does not change during the execution of the loop.

2. When all the resources on the computer are used up and it crashes. A restart will clear it out. Fix the infinite loop before you run it again!

3. As with the *if* statement and the *try:* and *except:* statements, Python requires a colon, :, at the end of the *while* condition.

4. Code belonging within the *while* loop is indented underneath it. To indicate that a *while* loop is done and a line of code does not belong with it, unindent that line back one level.

5. Add 1 to the variable *score* during each pass of the loop.

```
score = score + 1
```

This could also be written as:

```
score += 1
```

6. This code prints: Game over! The loop is never entered because the variable *lives* is currently 11, and it must be 10 or fewer to enter the loop. This is a zero-trip loop.

7. There are two ways to change the loop.

   One is to initially set lives to be 10 rather than 11.

   The other way is to change the condition to check for lives <= 11 rather than lives <= 10).

8.
```
count = 0
animal = input("What kind of pet do you have or \
do you want?")
while (count < 4):
   print(animal)
    if (animal == "gerbil"):
      break:
    count = count + 1
    animal = input("Name another kind of pet you \
    have or that you want: ")
print("Processing Complete")
```

9.
```
count = 5
while (count > 0):
    print(count)
    count = count -1
print("Blastoff!")
```

10.
```
while (number < 0):
    if (number % 2 == 0):
        print(number)
    number += 1
print ("Processing Complete")
```

11.
```
count = 0
numChannels = 1000
```

```
while (count < numChannels):
    count += 1
    if (channelGenre == "music channel"):
    continue
    print(count)
```

12.
```
count = 0
name = input("Please enter a name or 'done' \
when finished: ")
while (name != "done"):
    count = count + 1
    name = input("Please enter another name or \
    'done' if finished: ")
print("Total number of entries", count)
```

Repetitive Statements: *for* loops

1. Code that is indented under the *for* loop will be repeated each iteration.

2. As usual with Python, the colon, :, goes after the *for* statement.

3. Iteration 1: counter = 5

   Iteration 2: counter = 4

   Iteration 3: counter = 3

   Iteration 4: counter = 2

   Iteration 5: counter = 1

4. Next to last iteration:

   ```
   Locker#: 103 Elyse
   ```

Last iteration:

```
    Locker#: 104 Richard
```

5.
```
count = 0
for letter in "Mississippi":
  if (letter == " s"):
    count += 1
print(" The letter 's' appeared", count,
" times in the word' Mississippi'")
```

Functions

1. The word will show up in color in the Python IDE/IDLE. The programmer can then go to the official Python documentation https://docs.python.org/3/library/functions.html to see what it does.

2. A programmer can only use a built-in function in a program, not change it. This code is already written and tested. Only the executable machine code is provided to programmers to avoid changes to a built-in function.

3. A variable *cannot* have the same name as a built-in function. The built-in function has already reserved that word and has specific and documented functionality associated with it.

4. The keyword *def* is used to tell Python we are creating our own function.

5. As usual with Python, a colon, :, is placed at the end of the *def* statement.

6. Code belonging to a function is indented one level under the *def* statement. The first line of code that is not indented signals that the function definition is complete.

7. To execute the code in a function, you must call it in your program. To call it, the function's name is given + parentheses, and any needed arguments are included within the parentheses.

```
print("text to print")
calcAvg(score1, score2, score3)
```

8. Here is one possible solution. Assume the *temp1 – temp4* variables are already defined.

```
def calcAvgTemp():
    global temp1, temp2, temp3, temp4
    avg = (temp1 + temp2 + temp3 + temp4) / 4
    print("The average temperature was ", avg)


# Call to function
calcAvgTemp()
```

9. An argument passes a value to a function.

   A parameter is the variable in the function that receives the value from the argument.

   Parameters are local to the function.

10. Yes, parentheses are required with all functions, built-in and those we write.

11. A comma is used to separate arguments and parameters when there are more than one.

12. Here is one possible solution. Notice that I called the function with an integer 5, and a variable holding another integer 29. I could also correctly call it with two integers or two variables.

```
def avgTwo(num1, num2):
    avg = (num1 + num2) / 2
    print("The average is: ", avg)


number1 = 29
# Call to function
avgTwo(5, number1)
```

13. Variables defined in a function are local to that function only.

14. A global variable is available to the entire program.

15. To use a global variable in a function, use the *global* keyword and the variable name as the first line after the *def* statement defines the function.

16.
```
def myPets():
    global currentPet
```

17. Your function and variable names may be different, but the comparison in the *if* statement should be the same.

```
def maxNum(num1, num2):
    if (num1 > num2):
        return num1
    return num2
```

You could also have an `else: return num2` statement.

NOTES

NOTES

NOTES

NOTES

NOTES